The Changing Forest

Dennis Potter was born in 1935 and educated at New College, Oxford. His controversial career as a playwright, journalist and critic began in the 1960s. He was one of the first significant writers to write specifically for the medium of television. Although he was perhaps most widely known for the drama series *Pennies from Heaven*, for which he received a BAFTA Best Writer's Award, and *The Singing Detective*, his credits include almost thirty original plays, nine television serials, three novels, numerous works of journalism and several works of non-fiction. He died in 1994.

THE
CHANGING
FOREST

Life in the
Forest of Dean Today

DENNIS POTTER

Minerva

A Minerva Paperback
THE CHANGING FOREST

First published in Great Britain 1962
by Martin Secker & Warburg Limited
as part of the 'Britain Alive' series
This Minerva edition published 1996
by Mandarin Paperbacks
an imprint of Reed International Books Limited
Michelin House, 81 Fulham Road, London SW3 6RB
and Auckland, Melbourne, Singapore and Toronto

A CIP catalogue record for this title
is available from the British Library
ISBN 0 7493 8643 6

Typeset in Linotron Bembo 11 on 14pt
by Deltatype Ltd, Ellesmere Port, Cheshire
Printed and bound in Great Britain
by Cox & Wyman Ltd, Reading, Berks.

Author's Note

The Forest of Dean lies in Gloucestershire, west of the Severn and east of the Wye. It has been described as 'a little country on its own'. I was born there, and so was my wife Margaret.

I would like to dedicate this book to my father and mother, who live there.

I would also like to ask the people of the Forest of Dean not to be too offended about some of the things I have had to write, and the others who read this book to realize that it is only a part of the story, seen in personal and, maybe, argumentative terms.

Finally, it would be fair to express my appreciation of the encouragement and argument of four of my friends, Kenneth Trodd, Roger Smith, Robert Christopher and Michael Stevens.

FOREWORD

'Change' is one of the easy, dangerous words when applied indiscriminately to the atmosphere and life of a particular town or district: it is likely to make the observer concentrate on the hard outlines of surfaces, the shine on things, notice colours that were not there before, and hence also discover what have been called 'areas of unchange' where surfaces, colours, faces, streets and habits appear to have remained the same. Nevertheless, I have used the word in my title because I know the Forest of Dean as an important part of my own life, alternately attracted and repelled by it, rarely unaware of its power. I cannot write heavily charged prose to sing the praises of a city like Venice or Alexandria, and it may appear that, instead, I have chosen to labour over the minor or the obvious, or to encase feeling and description within the inconsequential walls of autobiography – but this must be the way to write about the Forest I know, smouldering within where its old culture is still alive, perplexing where the new has taken over. Only those who were born and nourished in a small, relatively isolated community can know how strongly the day-to-day shapes of the past merge into and appear to dominate the seemingly more uncertain contours of the present. 'More uncertain' because opening-out and new mobility, or new health, breaks up the old rigidities and attitudes, leaving them stranded as isolated, if large, blocks of ice in a slowly moving ocean of change. Or, to change the metaphor, it is a changing Forest of Dean, certainly, but with the old roads and coins of former occupiers only half-buried in a loose top soil.

ONE

I'll begin, then, with the old men, tired, mufflered, alien. To the old people, so much of the change is a peculiar noise they have to cup their hands to listen for – and therefore it simply isn't worth the effort. Instead, there is enough left, outside as well as within their memories, to live as always, apart from hardening muscles or creeping deafness. This whole sequence of residual habits strings across many of the older working-class parts of Britain and pushes its way into nearly everything which is apparently as brand new as an advertiser would claim – into songs, jingles, houses with contemporary furniture and schools made of glass. But with the old of the working class – or, rather, many of them – it has to be probed with care, and with fear, the kind of fear one has for settlers and immigrants in one's own land.

From where I was sitting, at one of the little square-topped two-layer tables along the wall on the piano side of the club, the talk of a huddle of old Foresters was just audible as a prolonged but broken low burr, penetrated by coughs, cackles of laughter and the shuffle of feet and chairs.

Shredded black tobacco twist stenched out a dark blue cloud to hang lazily over the bend of each head and shoulder before drifting unwillingly away to mingle with the sharper smell of draught cider. Looking across at them, completely unwilling to add the insult of sentimentality, I nevertheless had the strange but very 'creative' feeling that I could hold and feel the Forest of fifteen to twenty years ago, the Forest of my childhood. Conscious of my plans to write this book, returning home became something of a wrestle in autobiography, for things click too readily into place without the manipulation of 'objectivity' or the passive, necessary, but slightly distasteful business of 'standing apart'.

These older Foresters speak with a wide, beautiful splattering of chapel language, and use a hundredfold country and coal-mining superstitions and prejudices. They believe in God, in Britain, in the Forest and in the working class. 'Highsht!' they command to shut someone up − the Forest word for listen-with-urgency, and the Foresters listen without urgency, or even with the patent boredom of all who are afflicted with the old. So broad is the accent at its furthest limits that I doubt whether many outsiders would grasp two thirds of what was said to them, for it is a rich and very heavily flavoured mixture of the speed and lilt of the Welsh borderland, the broad, lengthened vowel sounds and buttery emphases of the West Country and many distinctive local words and rhythms of its own. Speech is still the easiest form of map reading for those who wish to explore England, but it is also the most difficult quality to capture in print. I usually dislike reading dialogue that is supposed to be in a strong regional accent, and, except to give an indication of its texture and pungency, I'll not attempt to convey the richness of this Forest speech: but it remains all the time, flowing through the conversations that went into the making of this book.

The dimensions given by hearing the words, as opposed to reading them, also gives one the thread of local change and the impact of altering assumptions as they affect the different generations. Strongly 'local' speech can be a sign of narrowness and isolation, and in speech, especially, the Forest of Dean is a jungle of change: already there is a tremendous, dictionary-like difference between the talk of the old Foresters and that of the younger people who are displacing them; not just in the choice of words, but in the way of saying them, the way language unknowingly breaks out from the inside of a person and echoes along the shifting boundaries of a community. Such changes as these can be extraordinarily difficult to identify, particularly when one is involved in them anyway: undoubtedly, though, a change of pace, of mood and direction has taken place.

Chapel (you can see one in each village, like a warehouse with tall, thin windows and a heavy door), rugby football, brass band, choir and pub: that's the old Forest, and, some will have it, that's the Forest now. All these things remain, and are talked about, but much in the same sort of way that Christmas is supposed to remain a Christian festival. Something far more of another order is replacing them.

I was brought up within this pattern, and certainly it was still dominant then, so recently have the new 'benefits' come to the district. Chapel twice on Sunday with Sankey's book of hymns, sitting on the window-sill when Salem was crowded and smelt of flowers of Occasion; lessons in the red tin hut of Berry Hill Silver Prize Band ('that's it, o'butty,

3

imagine thou's got a bit of baccy on thee lip and thou bist trying to spit it off, that's how to get the best out of a note,' explained the late Harry Baglin, a curly-headed, kind man who died comparatively young with silicosis, the terrible coal-dust disease which can choke a man to death), marching through Berry Hill behind the band as it showed the Salem Chapel banners round the village, waiting on the low stone wall outside 'The Globe', legs kicking, as they sang inside Bread of Heaven, The Old Rugged Cross and I'm Forever Blowing Bub-bools.

A way of singing always gurgles up from the stomach of the past, and one remembers incidental, diffuse things like the way the sky looked when the band turned the corner or the smell of the red hymn books in a pile on the back bench of Joyford Chapel or setting fire to a gorse bush in yellow flower. One must discipline 'the past' when drawing out comparisons with things as they are today. But the houses were part of the same picture of band, chapel and so on, extensions of it somehow. Now there seem to be new, well-designed council houses everywhere, sprawling over the stretches of gorsey ground between clumps of woodland. My village has easily trebled in size with whole new roads of aerial-topped, flush-doored, nicely painted, flat-windowed buildings with cars outside them and small pieces of lawn before you come to the front door. The older ones were square-looking, heavy things, built of local stone, bedroom windows half the size of the ones downstairs, big back gardens and a thick stone-walled pig's cot next to the outside lavatory. The lavatory had a long split wooden seat half the size of a park bench, built high over its smelly cargo, and for light a tiny window about the size of an average book.

4

Many of these houses remain comparatively unchanged, but most of them (whether in the pastel colour of the wallpaper, the bright paintwork, stripe of 'contemporary' wallpaper, tall flower vase, holding artificial blooms in winter, or in the television aerial, the built-on lavatory, with coloured toilet roll, and the concreted path) have changed, largely for the better. There remain, of course, rather like overgrown, unattended hedges, the cottages where elderly people live without any of their family, and quite a few where, through drink, laziness, ignorance and (more rarely) pride, the old habits and aspirations have not given way to newer expectations.

'Come in, o'but,' said one such inhabitant (I'm not sure which of the above reasons would apply), 'cast thee eyes over my abode.' He was an elderly man, with eyes gleaming remotely behind layers of creamy-coloured skin, and he still went to work. I should explain that 'o'but' is the more impersonal shortening of 'o'butty', and that 'butty' is a word used in most coal-mining areas for a work-mate, a pal and anyone within the group, with appropriately varying degrees of frequency and warmth. Some of the women kept calling me 'Mr Potter' even when they had known me as a child, and called my father by his Christian name; all of the men 'o'but' or, occasionally, 'o'butty'.

The old man was popular in the district, and he was a nice man, good to know. I had been talking to him in the lane, and he had, surprisingly, asked me in to show me an old and rather greasy photograph. As he talked, there was a rattle in his chest as if the mechanism which wound him up was beginning to break down, dust in its wheels. A horrible metaphor, I know, but I found it difficult to look him in the face for he clearly did not have very long to live – just over twelve weeks as it happened.

I stepped into a low, too crowded room which was smelling a bit of old age – rather like the faint odour of a room where a new baby has been sleeping and feeding – and waited while he rummaged around for the photograph in a shoe box on top of an old sewing machine. There were no coals in a big fireplace of four-barred iron grate, fronted by a long brass fender and set off with a mantelpiece cloaked in a brown tassel-frilled mantel-cloth. A grey streak of phlegm stained the bars of the grate, slightly luminous like the path a slug has made on its morning slither across a concrete path: silicosis spit, and a silicosis rattle in the chest. A cap hung on the shoulder of a fat old armchair, and the big clock on the wall was laboriously husky in its slow, almost painful tick-h, tock-h, tick-h. Beginning to slide back through the thicknesses of romanticism, I noticed a folded-up copy of *Reveille* on the table, although I could still hardly believe it. But there is no past complete in the present, even in such homes as this, although the conversation I had there was extraordinarily outside any changes in social habits or conditions. Yet again, I felt the power the chapels have had in these high, sloping, windy villages of Dean Forest. Inevitably, the conversation had got round to them.

I cannot remember the words he used, but the old man talked about the way the Bible had come to seem almost a *local* document to him, as real in its descriptions as any piece in the *Dean Forest Guardian* or any lump of memory. 'Thou's heard of the old saying, of course – blessed is the land between the two rivers.' The Forest lies between the Severn and the Wye, and a few miles from their confluence.

6

He expressed, without embarrassment or self-consciousness, that evocative power of passages of literature constantly heard or thought about to reach out and lay hold of pieces of landscape or patches of the day, so that a biblical passage begins to look, in a slow mix, like a particular place, and the place to sound like a paragraph, physically distilled out of familiar words. The Dead Sea, the dead sea, was the large dreary pond near a pit where he had once worked, edged with reeds, stones and scraggy trees whose roots twisted back to the surface like half-buried arms in a poisoned soil. Yea, though I walk through the valley of the shadow of death: trees again, barren-looking in a winter scene, arched at their black tops above the gauged-out lane falling to the bottom of little Joyford, an overhung, shadowy, stumbly lane where people walked quickly, whistling.

He talked quietly, and I had the uncomfortable feeling that this was the first conversation of length that he had had for a long time. Unused to words, there was still a response to these ones from chapel days, running their black edges together in an intense montage of feeling and imagination: the impression of immense unused and now unusable intelligence and sensitivity worried me, but that was a hard part of the old Forest as well – no chances, no sadness, little hope and one long grind. He kept opening and shutting his fingers as he talked.

'Of course it's all changed, butty,' he said, 'things yunt the same. You do what you're told nowadays.' I thought it a strange remark, but it may be true.

A step led up to the Front Room, preserved by a green door with a large, well-polished latch. 'Thoy used to measure my height against that,' he gestured, 'and I think

I've almost reached the bugger on my way downwards.' The Front Room has always been a holy of holies in such houses as these, a shrine to respectability rather than a place of retreat. If I was very good as a small boy my grandmother would sometimes ask me if I would like to sit with her awhile in the Front Room – this was an honour, qualified by 'but doosn't thou touch nothing, bless your little golden yud'. I am now tempted to divide houses in the Forest of Dean into those with 'Front Rooms', those caught in change with 'front rooms', and the larger, growing number with 'sitting rooms' or even, as a final emancipation, 'other' rooms. Here, up against a belt of wet trees, off the main road by a long puddly lane, I was in the Front Room part.

Front Rooms are rather unbelievable institutions: I know that some people take off their shoes to go in (men with Front Rooms would not consider slippers a possibility), and, once there, even talk a little more quietly, as if they were visitors in their own homes. The furniture is 'best', like a Sunday suit of clothes, the wallpaper is 'best', the cups, if a visitor is shown to the Front Room or a funeral procession should end there in stiff sadness, are 'best china', and the pictures are large and heavily framed. They may even include a portrait of Gladstone.

But when television came (how it did, I don't know), a decision of some importance had to be made: where did one put the set. Those early grey-faced, tall nine-inch sets – almost antique pieces now – were the most expensive, most beautiful and by far the most exciting things to be brought into the house. Unlike the old wireless sets, they created a fresh problem. They could hardly be put in the kitchen, even though that was where the evenings were spent, where the wireless was, and where the innumerable casual visitors and neighbours would see such an expensive acquisition, for cups of tea might be put on it, children might hack at it, and all the dangers of domesticity would engulf the bow-tied announcers and women in evening dresses.

And so the Front Room became, however reluctantly, a room for use. The little screen found its place amongst the cumbersome best furniture and the heavily flowered, deep-bordered wallpaper. And, of course, when the family began to watch, furniture got moved around, a few superfluous things were slung out, a giant change in domestic habits was being made. The first families to get television, who must already have had electricity and the ability to save, were anyway ripe for changes, and were already making them in other ways. Instead of a coal fire once a week 'to air the room', to preserve the mausoleum from the damp, fires were lit throughout the winter; some people even began to have a glass of beer or a flagon of cider, to keep on their working clothes and boots, consciously to relax over it all, to create a genuine living space in what had been the lifeless clutter of the old Front Room. When this happened, the former wallpaper was discovered to be irritating and out-of-tune, the best china 'a pity to keep for looking at', the heavily framed picture 'a bit miserable', and a minor revolution was finally consummated when supper was eaten in the room to the pale flicker of the Lime Grove light, eaten where once a mouse would have starved if it had to rely on the crumbs. I know several families in my village who have encamped from kitchen to front room in just this way. 'Home' as a word has shifted meaning – not only because of television and the invasion of commercialism through its so-called 'independent' channels, but because the whole background to Forest of Dean life has yawed into another angle. I must try to show how my birthplace is becoming to me, almost every time I return, less distinct and more like the rest of the country, gaining a lot in comfort and tolerance, losing a lot in cohesion, strength of community and what used to be known as 'self-reliance'. Around the Foresters, becoming a long way apart from them, and yet, somehow still their background and their inheritance, the old patterns are disintegrating so rapidly that one can almost *see* it in half an hour's walking and talking. Enough remains to reassure the older people, to quicken interest in the visitor and make him feel in a unique and lovable part of England, but I very much doubt if it can now be salvaged.

TWO

The first thing that a Forester asks of you is that you should say how beautiful the place is, no matter what the time of year. You would not find it difficult to meet this request, nor would you be immediately prepared to disagree with the claim that it is 'a little country on its own'. I know of few more fascinating areas, and, entering the Forest of Dean by whichever route you choose, you can soon sense that you are in a self-absorbed community where the inter-relation of landscape, work and the different generations demands more than the usual flickering attention.

Coming on the double-deckered Red and White bus from Gloucester – a city one would always want to get out of as quickly as possible – it is about twenty miles to Berry Hill, the large, sloping village in West Dean where I used to live. Only during the latter part of the journey does the bus enter the Forest where, suddenly, the road narrows as if dwindling off its regular route and begins to swerve and climb, while through the bus windows you can see that the climb will have to continue by stages, where large clumps of woodland

and high, sliding fields can be seen above the present levels. Tall straggly hedges lean inwards to smack against the top deck, and the green takes on a slightly darker, damper hue.

At the moment, the word 'idyllic' keeps intruding, irritatingly, and then forces acceptance. It really is very attractive. At first, the only signs of life, apart from the traffic itself, are a few dwellings which aspire to the status of farm houses, with apple orchards, a stream falling to the Severn, and, then, increasingly, some untidy-looking gatherings of squat houses, all with television aerials, now as universal and as unremarkable as chimney pots or curtains at the window. These first villages are linked to the outside by something swifter than the climbing roadway.

Yet the impression of comparative isolation lingers above the wire extensions on the roof tops; the trees thicken, so that as you glance at them, sweeping by, you can no longer penetrate so easily to the bumpy gorse ground or patches of fern separating the blocks of woodland. An occasional pathway breaks free and plunges spirally on to the green, and milk churns wait by the side of the road. 'Beware of Fire' say the Forestry Commission notices. This, now, is the tourist's Forest of Dean, as beautiful, surely, as any place on earth – richly wooded, heaving up in wide, green undulations, dissected by swift-running tributaries, most of which eventually reach the twisting, rock-dominated River Wye, and as distant as possible from the ugly excesses of the old industrialism or the concrete and glass slickness of the newer brand.

The names on some of the waist-high signposts might almost have been painted there by an inventive or tipsy copywriter employed by the British Travel Association.

There's Bream and Broadwell, Joyford, Hiller's Land, Speech House and Shortstanding, as well as Hope Mansel and Drummer Boy Stone. (There are reasons for all these names, from Clearwell to Nine Wells or Five Acres, and there is no need to be apologetic about them; the names of the roads on the new housing estates are more difficult to understand, for they are Surrey names, suburban names, grandiose names, like Edinburgh Place.)

This is the children's Forest, too. A place to collect birds' eggs and build secret cabins in the thickest parts of the Wood, to climb trees and search out and occupy abandoned quarries or old, disused pits, smelling with stale, silvery mud caked over the rusted rails. Adults, too, have always had this background and this release, and they appear not to take it for granted: surprise still revolves through the year – the myriad greens, the walks down an old stony road to the rapids, the bracken turning and crumbling into a dusty and universal golden brown, and, even in winter, the stark black trunks and icy stubble has its own bitter loveliness.

But I also remember sitting on the top deck of the bus, in the front seat, talking to a friend from London, and once again trying to explain the spreading, rising Forest scene as if it were urgently necessary to appreciate the rushing and exhilarating feeling of space and height, air and beauty, before beginning to understand and sympathize with the opposing tightness and stifle of close identity drawn into the villages straddling across the long, central and populous ridge of the Forest. The two things inter-relate like different views of the same scene, as if local speech and traditions were printed on the skyline, ready at any moment to fall like a cloak.

Half an hour or so after leaving King's Square in Gloucester, the Red and White bus begins the sharpest climb yet, crawling slowly up a long stretch of road out of Littledean, writhing with dangerous hesitation between banks of stubbly, dark green fields sliding off the crest of the hill. At the top, cringing backwards, are the first houses of the Forest's first town, Cinderford. But before the messy, narrow little town seeps up around you as the equally rapid descent compensates for the climb, a backward glance on the final turn allows an astonishingly thrilling glance of the now distant Severn, gleaming in unreality down below in stretches of farm land, almost as if it were one's first apprehension of what a river ought to look like, the apparent essence of riverness.

Cinderford, as its name might suggest, acts as an introduction to another, tougher and less obviously or willingly idyllic kind of Forest of Dean. Its houses, glinting grey, fall away on either side of a very steep and impossibly narrow High Street, nowadays always choked with traffic and delivery vans. There is a small cinema, a large war memorial with soldier and bayonet, a super-market (opened two years ago, the first in the Forest and, characteristically, owned by the Co-op), and it has now claimed the first Woolworths in the district. The familiar red and gold is part of the rush, as if the town had just been discovered lurking in its own past, ripe for what speculators call 'capital development' without conscious irony. Here, the bones of the old way of life are exposed alongside the plate glass windows stacked high with prosperity, frozen foods and brightly imploring hire-purchase signs. There is a new, candy-coloured shop called simply 'Do It Yourself', but one of the biggest buildings in town, overshadowed only by the Co-op and bigger even than the Miners' Welfare Hall, is a large, dusty hulk of a chapel, looking from a distance exactly like a riverside warehouse. It would appear to be ripe for a takeover bid.

The town still has a fairly good rugby side, a pale descendant playing on a muddy pitch of the Cinderford White Rose fifteen which played and beat some of the best sides in England and Wales during the first decades of this century. The failings of the semi-professional soccer team, which had to withdraw from the Western League for the less glorious backwaters of the North Gloucestershire Senior League, have led one local correspondent to complain that 'socially and culturally the Forest is failing'. and certainly a diagnosis from so narrow a front becomes more plausible when extended to other things. For instance, I can remember the gaudy carnivals in Cinderford, brassily led by Prize Bands 'from all over the Forest', in which each street sent its decorated float to compete with the rest. It was a day-long festival of brass and costume, drinking and speech making, where weird shapes bobbed through the squat grey streets as if to exorcize their dullness for the rest of the year. The two big pits nearest the town would release as many men as possible, and lose some of the rest, so that only the Christmas band-playing and party-going would seem more important or more releasing in the town's calendar. They have stopped the carnivals now 'because of the rain'.

In truth, though, it is difficult to know what the carnival would be like nowadays: excessively self-conscious, I expect, and soured by the knowledge that nothing so amateurish, so obviously inept when compared to glimpses of other ways, could possibly get by without a background of sniggers. There are no fat-cheeked Morris dancers here, and I would loathe them if there were. Coleford, another Forest town eight miles to the west, and much more pleasant in its general appearance, still celebrates an annual carnival, but it has become very different in style and impact, in a host of ways, being both more commercial and less spontaneous, a thing you pay to enjoy like the cinema. I found it rather depressing.

One particular homecoming I remember, when the cold had polished up the air until its glass reflection seemed to smack into one's face. I had to change buses at Cinderford and wait about thirty minutes for another to Coleford, a town thick with flanking villages, of which Berry Hill was one. Although my feet were aching with the cold, and Cinderford lay exposed to the wind like a loose tile or a punctured drain, I walked around for a few minutes before getting a hot drink. It was already dark, the early winter dark which would mean crumpets and talk in my big ugly room in New College (it was my first term), but here the widely separated street lamps fluttered a little in the wind, waving their sickly, yellowy pools of light to reveal too much grey and moving shadow to make one grateful for their existence. The thin light seemed to be letting in the cold, and complete darkness would have felt warmer.

To walk in Cinderford, especially in winter, is to share a little condescendingly in the town's sprawling mediocrity. The compensating life which tried to blot out the grey and the former poverty, which absorbed it as part of itself, has now changed scope and character; but the newer forms occasionally give the impression of the final and slyer triumph of the long-resisted flood of exploitation. I kept sensing posters, ogling windows, houses with people in them who were restless about how their furniture, their pictures, their standards appeared to other people. At the bottom of the town, I knew because for three months I had worked at it, men would be trundling heavy tubs of dough from under the mixing blades to a long waiting hall of shrouded tubs to await fermentation and manufacture into Meredith & Drew biscuits. Someone else, miles and miles away, would be writing a television commercial 'Yoo-OOH! Meredith and Drew-OOH!' They would be paid three or four times as much. And, as Herbert Harris told me, throwing salt into the fresh white flour, 'they don't belong to the Union here. They don't care about that sort of thing round here nowadays.'

Lower down, opposite the garage where I could get the second bus, I found a place to get a hot cup of coffee, and warm myself. The Telebar. During the day, the juke-box can be seen right up against the window, glistening through the reflections of cars in the glass as they glide up the hill towards the war memorial and the town centre. A girl with a cold nose, accentuatedly pointed breasts and a tight, shiny black skirt clicks her heels against the thick metal support of her high stool, and some youths are standing menacingly over the juke machine, slapping its sides impatiently, because this particular piece of heaven tends to stop and start arbitrarily, a result of jangling over-use and, possibly, former mishandling.

'If thou's ask me, thik box could do wi a good butt ash round the back on in.' A teenager with a leathery, fur-collared jacket and carefully dishevelled haircut had just

17

succeeded in getting his coin to drop with a clatter into the sleek fat belly of the machine. The grill-like, concave strands at the back began to revolve, and the arm came over with a click, hovered for a moment, a snake-headed bird, then, as if making an intelligent, considered choice, pounced swiftly on to the tiny black disc whirred into place by the machine, crushing it until it screamed with protest.

> *I'm ev-er so lone-ly bay-bee lone-ly bay-bee*
> *I-I could diiie!*

Sex, sex, sex. Sing to it, call for it, yearn for it. 'I got the UUUUUUrge for you, UUUUUUrge for you.' 'What will the teacher do, what will the teacher say, if she only knew, we were making love, mak-ing love, making lo-o-o-ve, making love.'

Originally, the owners of this little café had put in a television set on a high corner shelf above the counter at a time when they were still rare enough in the Forest to be a novelty. But now the latest occupier, the juke-box, was lord and master. The young people in the room jigged their feet and snapped their fingers, with something of the saving grace of self-parody, talking spasmodically in broad Forest accents.

A crumpled-up *Daily Mirror* lay across one of the few unoccupied stools, headlines aimed at the monosyllabic and the short-sighted. One of the cups littered around us was heavily smeared with orange-coloured lipstick, looking a bit as though it were fluorescent. The music had stopped again, and the talking spread out a little, heads moving together. Most of the people in the café probably worked at the new Meredith & Drew biscuit factory, built some time before in a

18

patch of woodland near to an old sawmill on the lower reaches of the town. Twenty years ago (army service excepted), nearly all the men would have gone to work in one of the pits near Cinderford, and the girls would have 'helped Mum', waited for marriage, or, still earlier, gone 'into service' as domestic servants outside the Forest or in the big houses further up the Wye Valley. Certainly they would have been poorer, less well nourished, more closely woven into the culture of the older generations.

'Did you go and see Terry Dene at Gloucester?' the black-skirted girl asked the two young men hovering above her, two she clearly did not know as well as she would have liked.

'What him?' Infinite contempt.

She flushed a little, and 'put it on' a bit to emphasize her dignity. 'Well, I think he's marvellous, myself.'

The taller youth laughed with a derision that sounded a bit too hearty, showing his interest as well, and there then began a series of remarks which, growing louder and louder and encompassing more and more people in the crowded Telebar, became almost a ritualized form of sexual combat. This was 'having a good time'. Words became strung out like a length of wire, twanging with too many meanings. Soon, they were all involved, throwing edgy opinions at each other, bringing in a kind of generally acknowledged hierarchy of Elvis and Tommy and everyone else on the pop market, and I began to feel pointedly engulfed by the talk. Lacking the energy, I could not peel away my shyness quickly enough, and left to catch my bus in the blustery and freezing main street outside the window. Here, at least, the juke-box made sense, and, perhaps, was preferable.

THREE

_____

Home is now a more private place, and 'community' more the public, distant word it sounds. People in the Forest of Dean, as elsewhere, keep more to themselves, go out further rather than less, lock their doors more firmly. Domestic intrusions are now of another, less tangible, more persuasive kind. The image of 'privacy' has become an ambiguous one, but must be used to indicate the new, seemingly withdrawn areas of domesticity.

Formerly, there used to be few places where you could escape the insistent beat of the Forest of Dean's sense of community, its totally encompassing and occasionally imprisoning way of life. It is of course true that much intolerance was bred in these coils of intimacy, gripping possessively at you should you happen to belong, pitying, despising or half-envying you if you did not. I confess that when I go back, which is very frequently, I still find myself – catch myself – deliberately restricting some part of my identity, difficult to locate, so that I am holding my tongue, as it were, genuflecting to something more collective. The result is that I both admire and resent the causes of such impositions and demands, but my life is no longer ruled by them in the same way it once was.

Until quite recently, and without choice, entertainment and leisure activities in the Forest were turned outwards in the individual case, but also inwards to the Forest of Dean itself, demanding and getting a communal response which was a heightening or a bolder colouring of the everyday, hard rhythms of living and working. It was as if a kind of collective solace had to be willed out of the unyielding fibres made up of dwarfed expectations and the quiet fatalism of 'things as they are'. It was a district borne up with the pleading but miserably passive sound of a hymn. The miners would walk home from the evening shift with carbide lamps or candles encased in jam jars, perhaps some four or five or six miles through the paths in the thick clumps of forest between the mounds of the pit and the lighted houses of their own village. On stormy or misty nights when the huge, gnarled oaks and beeches loomed up before their soft tread and black faces, trees dripping loudly with the perpetual night damp of the woods or howling in the wind as their tops swept to meet each other, the men would sing hymns or band tunes, eager to get home to the warmth and light, a bath before the fire, and bed. This was the world.

My father has told me of one such walk, on one pay night soon after he had started work at the Waterloo pit. He was very young and not especially self-confident after a severe attack of rheumatic fever. His butty and instructor was a much older man given to rampant superstition and speculation about who or what took over the woods when the sun had gone down and there was no moonlight filtering through the overhead lacework of high branches. The two of them had been delayed for some reason, and so separated from the main body of men walking on ahead, and his butty had had to abandon his carbide lamp as useless. The night was as black and as moody as only a night in thick forest can be.

Every twenty yards or so, the lamp replaced by 'a bit of comp' – a fat candle stump in a jar – the old man would stop, lifting his head to sniff like a frightened animal. A small, flickering arc drew round him as he turned to my father.

'Highsht!' he whispered, communicating some awful and hidden menace, 'Cost thou hear anything, o'but?'

Perhaps a twig had snapped, a branch creaked, or the dripping of the trees sounded too loudly upon the heaps of rotting leaves beneth; but my father, growing more and more nervous himself, would answer as contemptuously as he could.

'No! I can't hear anything!'

And they walked on a little further along the narrow path through the endless ranks of trees.

Stop again. The old man would ask, each time, with even more alarm and incredulity, 'Bist thou *sure* thou costn't hear nothing?' and my father, a little less convincingly, had to reassure him, insist that he could hear nothing unusual or dangerous, and, closer, they would move on once more, man and boy, breathing heavily, black-faced in the dark.

Then, at last, there really was a sound in the trees, a sudden rustle, prolonged into a swift retreating noise, obviously of some night animal startled by the two men. The old man lifted his stout thumb-stick as a warning.

'If ern a bugger do come near me I'll break his bloody head in two.'

22

The tremendous, loudly nervous way he said it made him sound anything but belligerent. By this time my father had become as frightened as the old man, and, without exchanging words, the two of them began to doubt whether they would get home safely. All the old Forest stories, the tales told to children, the mining superstitions related to danger at work, the country superstitions based upon isolation and history and religion, welled out of them to create an old and unknowable fear. Not until they glimpsed the lights from the first house windows and shouted 'good night!' underneath did the pressure lift from their foreheads.

My father, amused by it now, still tells the story with just a touch of lingering surprise that they should have reached home safely, and, for so small an incident, remembers and describes it today, more than forty years after the event, as if it happened the other day. It is (it was) a small part of the strong feeling of being 'a Forester', something complex and unique, something that outsiders were rarely expected to understand. There is a tremendously powerful clannishness about my father's generation which has not yet been broken down, and which the people of my age in the Forest find alternately amusing, irritating and admirable, only vaguely sensing a response shaped out of the former isolation, the poor amenities, the pits and their strikes and economic difficulties, none of which we experience ourselves. This response has hardened into the moulds of habit and is only now beginning to change.

It was (and, lingeringly, stubbornly, sometimes still is) an entirely male-dominated society. The women stayed at home, apart from the occasional Saturday night out, the summer band concerts on the common, and the chapel or pub outings to Barry, Weston or the Malvern Hills, smudged like a deeper hue of sky on the horizon. Their world must have seemed little but a pale glimmer slanted grudgingly off the man's activities, emptied of too much, confined by the cooking on big open grates, cleaning the metal fenders, drawing water from the wells or village spout, getting in the tin baths from the back kitchen walls, and sending their children to Sunday School with clean shoes and big white handkerchiefs.

For the men the 'we' was almost synonymous with the 'I'; they even had their holidays all at the same time, since almost all worked in the nearest pit. And the darker sides of the recent past came from this rough collectivity as well: contempt for any form of gentleness, for any feminine value, for any individuality beyond the permissible range. Those were also the days of occasional wife-beating and more frequent drunkenness, not quite so funny as Andy Capp's world (not general either, but sufficiently recognizable to suppurate into a permanent scar on many lives) – I can remember, as a child, clinging to the gate as a thin middle-aged or elderly woman climbed up the steep hill from Joyford, her awful face swollen and blotchy from tears and shame, half-shouting to a group of gossiping women in aprons that her husband had beaten her round the head with a bucket. I knew later that he was a very popular man in the village.

Home was looked upon, almost, as a place to eat, sleep, rest awhile and make love, or be imprisoned in when there was no money about, rather than the personal centre of a man's life and existence. And yet the home had to be 'a little palace' where 'you could eat off the floor and not have it cleaner', and where the Front Room was almost untouchable. No doubt within such a picture the women, those wonderful, over-worked, shapeless and prematurely aged working-class wives and mothers, were able somehow to create their own society within that allowed them by their menfolk, softer in its intent and less physically observable, less strident, than the male culture eddying around them in regular, monotonous predictability.

Nowadays, I think it is almost completely true to say that most people in the Forest of Dean, in the sum total of things, feel a greater sense of satisfaction and ease than they have ever done. Exceptions to this generalization will emerge more clearly as we continue: they are, briefly, the middle-aged men who have just left or are still in the pit, some of those just leaving school, the old (as everywhere), and the men and women who still cling to an old Forest culture, who run the bands, chapels, rugby teams and so on. And there are also the large numbers who have a faint distaste, or a thread of rebellion in them about what has happened. None who have experienced it are ideologically or cussedly romantic about the past, submerging the bad in it – which is inextricably part of the good – for the sake of clearer colours and attitudes; they simply cannot bring themselves to accept that the new society should be lauded as if it were the *only* and the *necessary* alternative to the old one which is falling apart and decaying as they grow older. Between all these groups and the more complacent exist the areas of tension and the leap of genuinely searching dialogue and argument. Always, in every part of Britain, there are groups caught up unwillingly or anxiously in the processes of change, being called upon to adjust their standards or question their values, putting graphic, personal meanings into the word 'change' or into the political platitudes and massed facts and figures of sociology.

A chapel preacher said to me, 'Look, young man, the only way to explain it in the end is that God is working his purpose out – it's like a change in the climate. The Forest must have had its summer.'

I nodded ambiguously.

FOUR

We travel in a bit further. The road between Cinderford and Coleford has one dramatic climb, known simply and aptly as the Long Hill in this region of hills, and fringed with massive old oaks on the one side and tender, newly planted trees on the other, opened out to reveal great bounces of landscape and miles and miles of forest. But before this hill is reached, the growing darkness of a winter's evening suddenly bursts into a row of light about a mile beyond the last ugly houses of the outlying Cinderford villages. Momentarily, it appears as a land-locked ship, port holes gleaming and engine throbbing from somewhere deep inside. By day, you can see the squat tower of a pit wheel and the pale blue N.C.B. notice which calls it the Northern United Colliery, locally just 'the Northern'. Up until now, the Forest has always hinted at something like this – the houses stand in stony opposition to the scenery, the people walking have that in their gait which is industrial, and you cannot fathom why Cinderford was built as it was, descending a hill. When the slag emerges from the bend in the road, it already seems natural, even familiar.

You can understand that the Forest of Dean was built on coal and lived or tried to live on coal.

A pit always dominates and terrorizes its setting, pulling the eyes with its ugly sense of power. 'I'da look at thik bugger sometimes, thou's know,' said one of my father's friends, 'and think – you bloody great sow!'

'Holt on, ol' un. Where ood we be wi' out um?'

'We shall soon find out that, butty. Too soon.'

They have found it out. Northern is now one of the last two big collieries left in the Forest of Dean, and is scheduled to be the last one to close and finally end a long, long chapter in the history of the district. When I last walked round by the side of the pit, men were raking over the hillocks of unsold small coal extending back a hundred yards and more from the road and the pit gates.

Further on a little, where the road begins to level out before beginning the huge climb of the Long Hill, there is another mucky-coloured slag heap, rising in decay and invaded along its lower slopes by some tenacious but ridiculous-looking plants. The heap has been thrown up over the years by the mine further down the slope, in the village of Upper Lydbrook. Here, one would have thought up to two years ago, the little square stone houses clearly depend for their living upon this big hole driven into the ground, for they cluster immediately below the pit buildings and machinery as if part of its outhouses, stables for its workers. There, too, in the midst of them, is the band hut, for Lydbrook is a great brass band village. The shift hooter cuts out the brass notes from the little hut and sends clusters of wood pigeons circling the trees in a fear they have never conquered. At least, that was how it used to be. The pit is called the Arthur and Edward Colliery, but throughout the Forest it is known by an older, and now ironical name, Waterloo. Arthur and Edward, apparently, were the names of the two sons of a previous owner, years prior to nationalization, and that in itself was a pretty good reason for the men to call it by some other name.

But Waterloo has closed. And in the Forest of Dean, as in many other parts of the country outside the Midlands and the consumer factories of London and the Home Counties, the same generation whose lives were so twisted and blighted by the depressions and strikes of the twenties and thirties is facing yet another challenge, another contraction and further indifferent talk about 'the necessity for labour mobility'. The labour force in the Forest pits has diminished rapidly, shifting the balance of work and income in this small community. An ageing band of miners is seeing the circle come swiftly and surely round to its full and unhappy completion. There are now only about one and a half thousand miners in the district at the time of writing, and two and a half thousand men have left the local pits in the last five years. The pits no longer rule the Forest, and although blue coal scars are common, and the mine is evident in talk and anecdote, the men of the district have turned elsewhere for their employment. The reasons for this are given briefly and bluntly in the *Revised Plan for Coal* of 1959, that unhappy epitaph for the hopes of so many mining areas throughout the country. 'Nye said he didn't want the pits kept open as national monuments,' said Harry Cooper, 'but how about making museums of people, then?'

The *Revised Plan* has one small paragraph, which states in its entirety: 'The Forest of Dean: This small isolated coalfield has a restricted market and most of the readily accessible coal has been worked. It is unlikely that more than one colliery will be in existence by 1965 and even this is dependent on demand. In any event, the greater part of the existing labour force will be unable to continue in mining employment in the Forest.' These sixty-five words have been enough to decide the fate of one of the oldest coalfields in Britain – and since they were written two more pits have closed, Waterloo and Cannop, leaving only Northern United and the Princess Royal collieries.

More than seven years ago, Aylmer Vallance warned in the *New Statesman* that 'the Forest of Dean is threatened with a local cataclysm'. Since then, remarkably little attention seems to have been paid to this timely warning. Vallance complained then that 'it is not enough to say that the Forest's future must be that of a tourist playground surrounded by a few ugly villages inhabited by employed young women and out of work old men'. But until a few years ago the posters beamed 'MINING – A JOB FOR LIFE', with the grinning thumbs-up miner confidently challenging the doubtful and those with memories of other times and other claims.

The *Dean Forest Guardian* (incidentally, a newspaper which seems to me one of the best small-circulation local journals that I have seen anywhere in the country, free of syndicated material and 'outside' ownership, and seemingly conscious of all the proper functions of the relationship between a newspaper and the area it serves) editorialized with some bitterness about the Coal Board's plans for the Forest: 'If anyone in the Forest of Dean had any illusions left concerning the prospects of the mining industry in the coalfield . . . [this] will have effectively removed them. . . . It would, we think, be wise for the Development Association of the Royal Forest of Dean to act on the assumption that some time before 1965, apart from a few gales worked by the free miners or under licence, coal mining in the Forest coalfield will have ceased,' and advises miners who do not wish to leave the district to 'accept without hesitation' *any* chance of other local employment.

But the question has been, what other local employment? When Eastern United Colliery was abandoned in the heavy snows of four winters ago, it took several months to absorb fewer than five hundred men. The older ones knew it to be a waste of time to queue for work at the local Employment Exchange. N.C.B. Group officials removed a holly wreath from the gates, put there as a final gesture of sarcasm and contempt, and expressed their regrets. The following winter Waterloo was closed, the act completed with a brilliantly thoughtful piece of timing to coincide with the Christmas holidays. Now the houses clustered beneath the old pit must send their men elsewhere, up the hill past the tall signs which say 'No Entry, Demolition in Progress'. Beneath Waterloo's slag heap, remnants of years of the old workings, one of the ramshackle checking huts has a glowing poster in its window which, complete with cuddly teddy bear, claims 'There is Nothing So Cosy as a Nice Coal Fire'.

Then, in the rainy summer of 1960, Cannop closed, so that three former centres were derelict, timbers rotting and pumps silent. The names of the five big Forest pits, Eastern United, Waterloo, Cannop, Northern United and Princess Royal, two of which will survive for a few more years, have been part of the local consciousness, of immeasurable significance in the life and vitality or hardship of the Forest of

Dean. When what prosperity there was, and even the situation and colouring of the sprawling, hilly villages and little towns of the Forest, had been decided mainly by the local mines, the few, bleak words in the *Revised Plan for Coal* came hard and painful to the people there. At least, it was assumed, their utter inadequacy might have been filled out with the platitudes expected of those who rule the lives of the miners.

I talked with many of the men who worked in the two pits nearest to Berry Hill, Cannop and Waterloo, most of whom I have known all my life. My father also worked at Cannop for nearly thirty years after he left Waterloo. At one time, practically every home in the village had a member of its household (and sometimes three generations) working in one or both of these two pits.

A streak of self-pity inevitably affected the way they talked about what had happened to the local coalfield. 'It was alright when we were wanted. National bloody heroes. Nothing too good, jokes about us on the wireless.' They realize that the N.C.B. carried on operations in what was fast becoming an uneconomic area – through exhaustion and dwindling seams – only because of the country's urgent need for coal in the years of reconstruction after the war. They remember that here, too, in a once poverty-stricken area, besides the 'guarantees' of the recruitment posters, came the insistent plea to the men to work a six-day week of full shifts and as much overtime as possible. This, it is acknowledged, would have been perfectly okay if, while time and opportunity had existed, a smoother, more human, and efficient rundown had been planned. But, as Oliver Oakey, a recently retired manager of Cannop told me, 'always they were on to us – coal, coal and more coal. It didn't seem to matter about anything else. Just coal – and we couldn't get enough for them, couldn't do enough, and no matter how much it cost per ton.' So the Forest, as always, had an active life only according to the state of the market for coal; good times alternated with the bad for this reason only. As a result, there is a great deal of scepticism about politics, including Labour politics, amongst the older people of the Forest, and the usual indifference of the young. And statements couched in high-flown and rhetorical idealism are greeted with scorn, with not even the polite shield of lip-service.

Through all the early days of the war, when work came back and the men responded to the slogans chalked on their shovels, and through the years of 'Export or Die' and the desperate winter of 1947, years when the miners were treated as heroes and medallioned giants, the decline of the Forest as a coal-producing centre (though scarcely whis-pered about at the time) has been 'as sure as God made little apples', as Jack Hawkins put it. Yet of 458 miners who lost their jobs with the closure of Eastern United, only 79 of these were promised new jobs by the Coal Board. No plans were made for the rest, and, since they did not want anyone to leave before necessary, as little notice as possible was given. Hence the wreath of holly, and the queue at the Labour Exchange.

And yet a place that thinks a lot of itself, that has a sense of its own identity, is frequently able to make nonsense of jaded descriptions of alleged apathy. There is, as a result, an astonishing air of liveliness about local councils and unions in the Forest of Dean, an illustration of a kind of reality about local democracy and concern that I had been inclined to doubt as a possibility. The district councils, tradespeople and unions formed the Forest of Dean Development Association in an effort to counter the too dangerous, too familiar limitations of long dependence upon a major industry with such a fluctuating record as that of coal-mining. The Development Association is not simply a paper organization, or a body working in isolation and without publicity or local concern, but something which has managed to be talked about, written about, argued about, praised and condemned with a vigour which shows how much it has been able to get a frustrated quietism turned into a rebellious and muscular concern about the continued life of the Forest as a place where it is nice to live and nice to bring up children. Most of the new factories in Dean have come about this way, with headlines of triumph in the local newspaper, motions of congratulation on the local councils and protestations of support and enthusiasm from the local trade unions. Part of this unanimity and energy may come from the fact that, by and large, the Forest is still a one-class area with a common accent and an extremely powerful, almost chauvinistic sense of its own values and traditions – 'our Forest humour', 'in this little Forest of ours', 'it's a little country on its own', 'once a Forester always a Forester'.

'If we don't help ourselves,' I was told, and it was agreed, 'nobody else will.' And while the Coal Board, for its part, issues a soothing but meaningless statement to say that 'the Divisional Board are deeply concerned about the position in the Forest coalfield', the miners continue to think they have been forgotten, made use of in the past, and then dumped like the unsaleable coal itself. They sense the confusion and lack of imagination that has settled in 'official' minds; for co-operation between the National Coal Board and the Board of Trade at a national level, and between the groups and Divisional Boards and local authorities nearer to home, has been and is far too shadowy to offer any real hopes of the planned resurrection for the area which might have taken place. The miners that are left, skilled through a lifetime at their own trade and ignorant of any other, are all too certain that the withdrawing Coal Board will be in no position to train the men, the ageing men, it is leaving behind; for, is it not obvious, coal miners have not given the same service to the community and are not as worthy of help as redundant and pensionable army officers.

Two summers ago, my father got out of Cannop, sick of a pit that had become swamped by dissatisfaction, rumour and counter-rumour, and managed to get a job at greatly reduced pay and much longer hours as a cleaner in the Red and White bus garage at Coleford. He was, comparatively speaking, fortunate to have been so placed, because he is in his fifties and avoided some of the rush of men of his age and experience which has weighed down the Forest over the last four years. But he finds his present job boring and irksome in a way that, as far as he is concerned, mining could never be. Pushing a broom along the ridges between the bus seats, he describes it, where once he had listened for the slightest creak, the ache in the timber long preceding any movement in the roof above the stall: mining certainly engages a man's attention, and gave moments of pride, while the hate for it was not the contempt he is now enduring in his new job.

Mining was possessive, and bred its own ethic. The ex-miners in the Forest of Dean miss this, and find it difficult to pin down their exact objections to factory life or other work.

'The trouble is, you know,' I was told by the Personal Assistant at a local factory, 'these miners are difficult chaps to employ. Always ready to make trouble, and they find it difficult to settle down to factory life.' Brown overalls for those on maintenance, 9 a.m. for staff, 7.00 or 7.30 or a shift system for 'the workers', a divided canteen, a factory magazine which is, of course, an employers' magazine, a weakening of Trade Unionism and the atmosphere of individual promotion, the faint possibility of individual bargaining – all this is felt to be deeply obnoxious, a trap. The miner does not believe in 'emancipation' through individual grace or annual bonus which is a percentage of annual wage. The younger Forester, however, is not altogether so sure about 'our side' and 'their side', about 'us' and 'them', and is not so conscious of his bargaining-power either. There has been a considerable decline in the political consciousness of the area, as shown in the flavour of the talk and in the faint but discernible mental shrug with which the older concepts of 'working-class' ambition and purpose are met. 'It's no use,' I was told by an acquaintance from Mile End, 'I can't talk to our old man – he's always on about this or that, about what we're supposed to be cheated of, that I just give up.'

Meanwhile, those who still work in the pits, mostly middle-aged men now, continue to squat on the village crossroads to wait for the workmen's bus which takes them through the trees to the mine. At Berry Hill, a few wait on the corner opposite 'The Globe' with its Ansell's Beers sign and yellow-wash walls, and the signpost which says 'Joyford ¾'. They wear mufflers and caps, and there is that washed-out paleness on the older faces, the blue coal scars, and 'bread' in old Home Guard or army satchels and Oxo tins. A way of dressing, the kind of stance, has already begun to date them: the young Foresters do not squat on the backs of their heels as these do whenever they have to wait. These miners are some of the men who laid the huge and attractive Berry Hill rugby football and cricket ground during the 1926 strike, whose minds are full of memories and talk of rugby, the band or the chapel or Coleford's Fair Day. But they are not posing for a photograph, for they themselves have willingly changed, or drifted along with it like everyone else. Behind them, Hawkins' Stores, now a limited company, is building a new extension, serving the young families in new council houses up the road, offering Danish blue cheese, telly snacks, striped toothpaste and coloured toilet rolls.

For a moment, if you did not visit them at home or talk of other than traditional subjects, the men outside the shop might appear to wait like monuments, carved out of the thick substance of the idea of a miner, the idea of the twenties and thirties, so that they will seem, almost, to be statements that have been completed, expressions that are no longer relevant or certain. A charabanc on the way to Symond's Yat Rock, jutting out above a loop in the Wye, whirrs past the mediocrity of the village; but the visitors inside it, heads back against the padded top bulge of the bus seats, stare for a moment at the groups of waiting miners, place them in the newspapered recesses of their minds, and wait for 'the scenery' to reappear once more. 'Hold it!' a voice seems to shout. Snap. And we are safe again with Andy Capp, or 'working-class' poses, or easy political claptrap from right and left angles.

Yet there can be no such docketing and filing away, no area of 'unchange' and little relevance or adequacy in former words and attitudes that described the miners. Albert Brookes, of Bream, can describe how when he used to work at Princess Royal colliery, he and some of his butties 'were a danger to the owners because we believed in nationalization. I don't regret what I did then, but the owners said that I should not work in a colliery again, and I did not. Even a member of my family was refused a job because he bore the name of Brookes.' But now nationalization has come, thug-like victimization has ended: what New Jerusalem is there, then, to overtake the old bitterness, the old political vigour and purpose?

'Nationalization' was once a magical, a golden word, a touchstone, to the miners of the Forest of Dean, but now the qualifications and the doubts, the confusion and the straight, emphatic rejections cloud the original optimism. 'Gratitude' is rightly a grossly reactionary concept when demanded of others as a result of what nearly always turns out to be marginal change. Now the men talk of 'being ruled from Cardiff', giving a fresh edge to the traditional antipathy of a border people for the Welsh, who are dirty at rugby and shut their pubs on Sundays; of officials who arrive in gleaming black cars to arrange a football match, and of other administrators who have the same faces and the same smiles they had before vesting date, nearly fifteen long years ago.

There are plenty of signs left of a goodwill that has otherwise been squandered, destroyed not so much by indifference or heartlessness, but more from a failure of nerve and imagination and the bitching of newspapers combined with the delaying tactics of successive Conservative govern-ments. (I would certainly not deny, of course, that within the limitations of the statutes, the Coal Board has had a difficult job in the mining areas, both attempting to counter old hostilities and resentments in the effort to build at least the outward show of a new spirit, and to meet the clamorous demand for higher and higher production with a shortage of manpower for all tasks. The N.C.B. has undoubtedly brought great improvements, largely in ways one never reads about: confidence in stating a grievance, brighter canteens, more realistic wages, safer conditions, treatment less arbitrary and hardly ever vindictive in the old sense.) 'They used to say the pits belonged to us,' said Jack Hawkins with heavy sarcasm, and there was a shout of laughter round the table.

'It's my opinion that our union was gulled by nationaliza-tion from the start,' Finlay Maclean thumped, cap pushed belligerently back on a handsome head, large fist clenching on the table. 'We ought never to have agreed to work the six-day week, to go flat out. Look at us now. If I had my way, we'd all refuse to pay our Union dues. Anyway, this is a Labour area, and always have been, so we shan't get much change now, you mark my words.' It wasn't long since he had taken out a mortgage on his house, still sure that the posters had told the truth, but now he was coming to expect a future period without work or on a very much lower weekly wage, so that the mortgage was likely to be a dread and a liability instead of the opportunity it had seemed to be for him and his growing young family. Jack, who used to play the hefty euphonium in Berry Hill band, his foot strapped up for a while from a pit accident, thought it was time 'to throw the buggers out and have a revolution like the workers did in Russia. We've been told too many things for me to listen any more.' He certainly isn't a Communist, nor particularly interested in the ramifications of the wider field of politics, but was simply using the newer sounds of bewilderment and frustration. How did they, how *could* they, change these things? Had they not been told, in the heady, fashionable radicalism of the time, that the pits 'belonged to them'? This was the phrase that rankled.

It's no use, and would be suspiciously hypocritical, to tell the men squatting for the workmen's bus at Berry Hill Cross that they had hoped for too much, had taken slogans too seriously, when 'the nation' took over from the coal owners. I remember, one day-shift tea-time, soon after nationalization, my father, home from Cannop with some blocks of wood for the fire, had talked and talked over the food, a thing he rarely does at length since he was brought up, as was usual, to believe it very rude to talk at the table. Usually we would stop serious gossip when the cook was ready, steaming on the table, for tea-time on day-shift was almost as important as Sunday dinner. This particular time must have been during the first few weeks of the take-over, when the blue N.C.B. flag was just a promise as yet, and still a surprise. Obviously, I cannot recall exactly what was said, nor even the way my father's face was set while saying it, for I was only eleven years old: but I do distinctly recall the optimism, the rather aggressive sense of satisfaction, the constantly reiterated glow of 'things are going to be different from now on'. And, most of all, I can remember this being accompanied, as if symbolically, by gravy being mopped off the plate with a piece of bread, as if removing the past with a few quick, cleaning strokes of the hand.

I was in my second term at the grammar school in Coleford at the time, and I think that that long winter, when snow brought the lanes up to the level of their hedges and marooned whole villages, provided my first genuine emotional and mental involvement with adult talk and hopes of politics. The atmosphere of confidence and something approaching trust was inescapable, and provides a great contrast to the more comfortable atmosphere today: the war had been won, our government was in, and they were starting to build houses again, beginning with lines of white boxed prefabs at the near-by village of Broadwell. Such things were probably beginning to dominate conversation, for they certainly crashed through even to the minds and talk of children in a way that seems weird and impossible today. All around us, the grown-ups were as if reaching out with their fingertips, feeling for the limits of this new world, buying things that would have denoted almost a middle-class existence a decade or two previously (although still not cars, radiograms, wall-to-wall carpets and blue cheese).

The years immediately after the war stand out clearly as the nearest point of reference to the old Forest culture at its fullness, although even then it must have been pushed gradually towards the defensive. I write this with caution, for nostalgia soaks over childhood years, and only after listening to others and piecing evidence together. It is strange that those years are difficult ones: the fuel shortage, rationing, 'Export or Die' warnings, physical controls and so on; yet, badly as such things may have affected and disillusioned the middle classes, those years when set against what had preceded them were also pretty satisfying ones for the older, once depressed working-class areas, particularly where mining was the staple work. Everything was then being cleared and tidied to light the bonfires which ended the war.

The boxes of ammunition were being removed from the thickest parts of the wood, where it had been stacked with mustard gas; the Italian and German prisoner-of-war camps at Broadwell were being closed, and the soft-booted Americans had returned, for the time being, to their homes, leaving behind a few hybrid Foresters, some massive trucks with blunt noses and big white stars, as well as many straight, jeep-wide paths of red ash cutting through the woods. The rugby team was having a couple of successful seasons, with the crowd numbering in several hundreds ('the touchline was black with people, o'but,' said Stan Adams. 'Now if it was Cardiff or the Harlequins up there you oodn't get more than a handful. I don't know what it's coming to – used to be one of the biggest things in the village.'). The chapels were full, so that we younger ones would occasionally have to sit on the window-sills because the benches were filled shoulder to shoulder. 'It seemed like a relief from war,' said Bert Harris, the Salem preacher, 'the whole place was picking up again. Then gradually the drift away started.' The band got new uniforms with brighter buttons and buckles, some new instruments and Boosey & Hawkes music cards, increased its concerts and marched regularly through the village. There was plenty of work at the pits, and plenty of trade in the pubs. The carnivals were successful and there was still little traffic on the roads, no television, juke-boxes or new-style coffee bars.

I cannot, of course, know how widespread or deep the feelings of optimism and self-assurance were, whether individually or in the bigger, more predictable life of the community: but this was, I feel fairly certain, a time when the way of living, the roundness of the Forest, was sufficiently whole to be held in a man's mind. Loyalties and traditions, hopes and assumptions, were precise enough to be manage-able, insofar as they ever can be, and the line weaving in and out of people's dealings with each other was a bit stronger and less broken or threadbare than it seems to be now, in 1961.

A strong sense is given to me, able as I am to keep returning and measuring my birthplace, of the way that nowadays the men and women of the Forest, as elsewhere, act as though they are tuned in to a different wavelength from the older ones, picking up, with new equipment, a different set of personal and social priorities. All of us there talk more in a sort of second-hand way, and most of us are hesitant or apologetic about our beliefs and habits: the animation of the old culture has dwindled away into a more evasive, less immediately tangible way of communication. The pages of the *Daily Mirror* flutter, the flashing star of an ITV 'natural break' explodes on the screen, the closeness of pit work is broken up and scattered amongst a few new glass-receptioned consumer factories.

And in the damp grass of a warm evening I saw an image which seemed to me to be full of this kind of change: a youth, in bluey, tight jeans and a conscious, almost painfully copied nonchalance in his chew-style walk (if you know what I mean) crossed the grass to the road with a transistor radio held like a biological specimen on the crook of his open hand. Less than a hundred yards away, the band was playing, having turned into a ragged circle, and a woman was sitting on a mackintosh, chewing sandwiches. The radio sent out gusts of a particularly phrenetic rock, laced over the sound of brass. The youth, in whose face I had already recognized the

43

gormlessness of an older man I knew, shouted across to the sandwich-muncher: 'Can you tell the difference?'

'Eh?' she bellowed back, her mouth full of whatever it was.

'Stork! Stork!' he jigged, 'it's easier to cream!' and, laughing like a fool, he reached the road.

'Crinkle', an old bandsman with a tight fuzz of grey hair, uncurled himself from the wall which was on the far side of the road. He was trying to listen to the band, sucking in his breath every now and then as he detected a wrong note, a late entry or a slurred intonation.

'Shut thik thing off, ol' un,' he said.

'Oy, putt n' off, o'but,' said another voice, further along the wall, 'we came out to listen to the band, not to thee.'

The transistorized youth was moving off, anyway, so he turned the set up, defiantly.

'Boiingg!' we heard the interrupting hammer-stroke of Radio Luxembourg.

'Crinkle', with his fist held low, charged after him. 'Putt the bugger off!' he spat, 'station of the stars!'

The boy was, of course, too quick for the old man. Laughing, he made as to sprint up the road, away from the band, still booming away across the common, and from us.

'Listen to the band!' he shouted back, 'you'll get stiff in the marnin' chasing after me.'

'Go home, you silly little bugger. I'll warm your ears up for you.'

Waving a contemptuous farewell, the youth strolled off, the sound of his portable radio disappearing as the band re-established its ascendancy.

'I don't know what the ploice is coming to,' panted

44

Crinkle, getting back on the wall. He had just lost his job in the pit, and, clearly, he thought things could never be the same again.

FIVE

Berry Hill, being one of the larger villages in the central, high and most populous ridge of the Forest, has two chapels, one a Methodist outpost, Zion, and the other a 'free church', Salem. Zion and Salem, Salem and Zion, twin guardians of the village, not above a great deal of jealousy for each other; and at times in the past, their associations were as much social and political as narrowly biblical, for this form of Christian fundamentalism has often been closely related to the history of the English and Welsh working classes, and our Labour movement. Salem and Zion were once, undoubtedly, the two most important places in the village, revered far more than the band and the rugby team. Their prim stone hulks were the solidification of almost everything judged important in the life of the district gathered immediately around them. Half a mile away there would be another chapel, and, half a mile onwards again, yet another. Each a ruling centre, with a ruling cabinet and a discipline as immutable as an established natural law.

Such crowns as these have felt the changes of the last

decade more than any other part of their kingdom of the collective, old-style existence: their decline has not been due to a change in intellectual assumptions about God or religion, for there is a common 'acceptance' of these imponderables, but to the gradual drift away from the demands and habits of the old Forest of Dean. Zion and Salem are now rather ugly memorials, as if to victims of a forgotten or unpopular war, placed in important positions, but neglected and not even in the eye-line any more. They are really alive in the old sense only when thronged with small children at Sunday School or anniversary time, but even then it gives one the vague disquiet of seeing infants playing in a churchyard.

Salem is the smaller and neater of the two, because Zion has a small balcony, where Salem has none, and looks half as tall again from the road. There is a mild, not altogether explicable social difference about which of these two chapels you would most naturally wish to attend – or, at least, there used to be in days gone, for such details as this have been obliterated by a new and far larger status: if you attend either, whether shopkeepers' Zion or 'popular' Salem, you are in any case part of a minority, respected but still dwindling, and growing older. The same goes for the Churchgoers, for Berry Hill is also in the parish of Christchurch, a squat, single-belled tower of the Church of England, lonelier now that the one-storeyed, ramshackle school with earth closets has at last been locked up. Chapel and church were not necessarily in direct conflict, for the church is used by chapel families for christenings, weddings and burials, as well as the occasional special service, such as a Harvest Festival.

When I used to go to chapel, as a boy, Salem and Zion,

and the host of others with similar names, were still clinging to their status and influence, and their past did not seem startlingly different from their position then. And yet, already, the past tense was being used, and language was beginning to hint at change: the former days of Salem, for example (the glory days), were described with more colour and certainty, making them seem so much more volatile, peopled by bigger and stranger elders. As so often happens, the greater stability, the greyer habit of the present became a prelude to the indifference of a few more years forward into the nineteen fifties and to today.

Chapel preachers of old are talked about in the Forest of Dean with an intensity and frequency which shows that they would not be tolerated today, rather as any social unit builds up a type of nostalgic orthodoxy with which to place and feel itself as something with a specific and valuable sense of identity, never quite able to see that such an orthodoxy bears little or no relation to the conflicts and growths of the present. In Berry Hill, at least, a few of the old local preachers have long since been elevated to the legendary, or promoted to glory as more determined evangelists would have it. But the legend has little to do with their devoutness and religious zeal, more to do with a questionable hell-fire vigour and humour, much of which was alleged to be accidental. Many of the reputations were fed, of course, by colourfully apocryphal stories and outrageous rumours, but, always, they reflect the realization that this apparently grim nonconformist Christianity gathered into itself all the prejudices, foibles and character of the region, becoming the reason for social gatherings, debate and enjoyment as much as the occasion for lessons and moralizing about the beauties of

God and the slyness of the Devil, or the iniquity of one's fellow men, certain colliery owners in particular. These chapels were class institutions, exercises in self-expression and a righteous *collective* ambition.

I have long been fascinated by the stories of preachers, by their wide currency and affectionate intent, and I think it is in place to give just a few of them. For me, there is the kind of Christmas, fireside, dead-of-winter story quality about them, and stories are part of a community's heritage, or a community's development.

At Salem, nearly all the so-called 'visiting speakers' came only from as far as some of the nearest villages round Coleford, such as Broadwell, Joyford, Coalway or Edge End, but they would always begin by making the appropriate deferences to the character and renown of Berry Hill. ('Wherever we go, we're happy you know, for we are the Berry Hill Boys, the Berry Hill Boys.') They were usually men who worked in the local pits, and in other circumstances and different times some of them would surely have become writers, poets or actors as well as political hatchet men. Yet they also thought of themselves as emancipators not of themselves, but of their class; not as 'better' or 'more qualified' or entitled to more material things, simply as chosen specialists, performing a major social function after a fashion which would help sharpen and purify the institutions and dignities of working-class culture.

And so the chapels found themselves providing adult 'bible classes' which were, in effect, centres of further education, since any problem, whether of evolution, imperialism or the unyielding 'coal question', could legitimately (and, in their eyes, must necessarily) be yoked into passionate and full-scale discussion of religion and morality. Heads would bend over the tall oil lamps, benches would be pushed together, groups would linger outside the chapel before walking home through the lanes, and the language of the bible would swell out into political terminology, Jewish history into the hopes of twentieth-century English coal-miners. Links such as these leap out for recognition should you happen to read or listen to the speeches of some of the older Union leaders. They have, in their texture and their finality, an almost biblical ring, echoing with foreboding and familiar words like 'doom', 'sin', 'evil', 'charity', 'as men one unto another, each of the other'.

'I doubt, because our leadership ignores the strongest foundation stone upon which all Socialist principles are based ... yet to judge by the sayings of our leader, they preach the opposite.'

'We have gone deeper into the mine by accepting *hidden allowances* – a complete charity; and charity, from the Coal Board, covers a multitude of sins. The sectional strikes that are now occurring with monotonous regularity, are the sins calling for retribution.'

'The few enjoy the benefits of production and the many get the curse of overtime.' And 'Raise your voice against this damning and undemocratic "yardage" method of payment – a system so saturated with greed that it would corrupt John the Baptist himself!'

The above were taken from *The Miner*, a Union magazine. The local newspaper provides scores of such examples, but I have no copies by me as I write, so you must take my word for it. You will not, however, find any of the under-thirties using such language, or even many of them

50

expressing beliefs in any wide-ranging form at all, for codes and hopes appear more fragmentary.

Socialism itself, in chapel language, in offshoot Union language, was often made to sound like the fitting reward on earth for a life of virtue and labour, a life to which capitalists and blacklegs enter as camels through the eye of the needle. My grandfather once claimed that 'there was as good among the rich as there was among the poor', and was immediately silenced by an appropriate quotation. The black-and-white rigidities of such fundamentalism, whether this kind of Christian or Socialist, or a mixture of both, have been muted into softness and unimportance or ridiculousness by the changing ambitions and declining fears of the people of the Forest. They have moved on to another political situation which is more difficult to express; but where, as always in working-class communities, people are still attempting to grapple with it. But the old dynamism of language has not kept up with an essential similarity of situation as revealed in terms of conflict and growth, friend and enemy. Now grandiloquence on the old chapel scale seems futile and rather embarrassing, and, just listening, it would seem that the Forester is no longer so sure (or so keen) that he is marching to Zion, beautiful, beautiful Zion, wonderful city of God, or the land of 'brotherhood and equality', at least to judge by the road now petering out into a brushland of immensely careful, properly cautious qualification, apology and doubt – above all, doubt. I think of the waiting miners again, and of *Reveille* in the old man's kitchen. But, again, the old Forest of Dean culture remains, for me, and a whole generation, too narrow, and that's pretty certain – the 'ultimate' Zion cannot have had its streets paved in final form in all those years of poverty and fear.

Salem chapel is now in the charge of Mr Bert Harris, a miner, who also runs the Berry Hill Scout troop and has for many years been a member of the village band. For him, at least, it would appear that the older Forest life is still as real as ever: in fact, he must give up many hours a week to those pursuits, another of the fast-diminishing number of people who tinker and polish and coax the old machine into running order. They will have no successors in the same complete and, one might say, dedicated manner.

Mr Harris has a hint of a carefully yet not sufficiently hidden melancholy in his features, perhaps a gentle and personal comment on his own situation as he sees it. He has neat, silvery hair, an energetic but immensely dignified grace of movement, neat hands and a face one can best imagine reading a well-bound and slightly musty old volume. 'Good', when applied to a whole person and not a particular deed or ambition, is an indefinably awkward and almost impossible word, trembling on the derisive or the banal, but it is a word often awarded to Mr Harris, and I choose to use it myself as well. He expresses many of the things which are most fine, and yet which are most on the retreat, in that older culture of the Forest of Dean, and even now, a kind of innocent (nearly gullible) patience makes him wait, still certain that there will be a return, once again a need, for what he believes and lives by.

I saw him after a meeting, and, drawing his hand half across his face as people do when they are tired but still wish to concentrate, he confessed that nowadays he often got to wondering whether it was any longer worth while trying to keep the chapel open; whether, indeed, the whole apparatus of the Forest life he used to know, with chapel prominent, was not crumbling away, slowly, with many protestations of respect and regret, but inexorably. As sure, he might say, as God made little apples. I asked him about the children in the Sunday School classes, and the young 'learners' in the local bands (Coleford Town Band, for instance, has the largest number of boys in its ranks in its history), for, on the face of it, there must have been something here to encourage him, to make him believe that patience would be rewarded. But no. 'They are sent to these things by parents who don't really want to cut their children off from the things which once seemed so important to them. I suppose they look on it as a kind of duty. But, I've seen it happen time and time again over the last few years or so, as soon as these children reach what they think to be grown-up stage – fourteen, fifteen or a bit before sometimes – they just don't want it. It's not enough for them any more – down to the café, a few records, and so on, that'll do now.'

I think it is true that the children are sent as hostages to the parents' own past, rather as a few Welsh people living in London have their London-accented children taught Welsh. The genuine continuity, represented in a full intercourse between the generations on the same terms and assumptions, has disappeared. Why then keep working for the chapel, the band, when these seem to the adults to be as lingering drops of an almost unbearable nostalgia? 'Someone will want it, sooner or later. We've got to keep going, that's all there is to it – we've got to be there, ready.' But I think he will continue to be disappointed.

On two successive Sundays I went first to Zion (now

almost surrounded by the new, pleasantly designed council houses) and then to Salem, where I had gone as a child. At Zion, the Methodist chapel with the balcony, there were eight or nine people, all but two over the age of forty. A woman preacher talked for a bit too long and a little too belligerently about 'our community under the Lord Jesus', and the small flock was asked, a trifle desperately, to pray for the others who had decided not to come. Maybe it was because the last dirty streaks of snow were on the road outside, making the chapel cold and draughty, but even in better circumstances I could not believe that 'the flock' would ever again be very large for the ordinary week-to-week services, nor would it have many representatives of the young to middle-aged adult villagers. The collection box made me feel rather as if I was giving money to some hopelessly small and eccentric sect, on a par with the Hartlepools nudist group or the Texas vegetarians, until I looked again, clinically, at the old people in the tiny congregation sitting bolt upright on the hard benches, and felt ashamed, if still a bit irritated. I had remembered the chapel heavy with the quiet shuffling and coughing of a packed congregation.

Going back to Salem was a stranger, more involved experience, discovering a building, a pulpit and windows shrunk from the measurements of recollection. Yet physically nothing seemed to have changed – only in the filling-out of the building, the numbers there. Before, I could not remember seeing it even half empty. This time, however, there were but ten or eleven people there, enough for two and a half benches to be partially occupied, a congregation scattering itself in an effort to keep privacy or to protect itself from its smallness. Again, they were old. Their brief whispers sounded old. One had a deaf aid and the suggestion of a body tremble, and another's hands, clinging to the hymn book, were club-like with the painful swellings of arthritis. Often in the Forest I have tried not to hear the phlegmy, sharp coughing of those with silicosis from the years of coal dust, but I couldn't get away from it this time.

But when Bert Harris announced the number of the hymn, they all stood up, and sang with surprising, throaty vigour, so that from the road outside, still sloping, it must have sounded as though the chapel was nearly as full as it always used to be.

> *Onward Christian soldiers, marching as to war*
> *With the Cross of Jesus, going on before!*
> *Christ the royal master . . .*

Mr Harris maintains that it is only within the last five or six years that the chapel has seriously felt the impact of the changes in the Forest of Dean, very rapidly losing its major significance in the village, but that decline in membership has been a more gradual and less startling process. The past was now more important to the chapel than thoughts of the future.

'You used to know what time they'd come,' Mr Harris continued, 'and where they would sit. It used to be a great social occasion – talking afterwards, meeting people, helping each other, going off to tea. And some speakers would draw the crowds just as if it were a football match – great characters, some of them. Great characters. But I can't even get good visiting speakers now, they aren't being bred up from the young ones any more. Nobody do seem to know how to talk like they used to.'

I've heard a lot about these 'great characters' from the past, enough to know that the description is at the very least a justifiable one, for they had a tremendous and sometimes unfortunate range of imagery (a persisting Berry Hill story is about the preacher who maintained that what he had been saying was 'as clear as the glass in thik clock', which must have exceeded all clarity since Salem's clock had no glass in it at all), as well as a sweepingly vituperative rhetoric and unashamed political vigour and polemic. As I have indicated, the sermon had to be an opportunity for something far wider than the conventionally hushed, rather quietist message of modern Anglicanism, a place to agitate one's fellows. It also produced more than its expected share of humour.

My father has told me about one particular preacher, a little, stumpy man with an evilly hooked nose, who was called Emmanuel and who had to supplement his height to reach pulpit level by standing on a margarine box he used to bring with him. His humour was frequently unintentional, for a windy command of rhetoric would sometimes force him into the most wildly unexpected similes.

'The world is as round as . . . as round as . . . as . . . as . . . as as . . . a horse's yud!'

A dreadful silence followed, where even the heavy tick of the clock appeared to be on the edge of whirring into croaky laughter. A few ladies hastily searched out their handker-chiefs. Emmanuel stood still on his margarine box, flushing with the realization that the triumphant flourish of discovery which had ended his momentary stuttering was not after all so triumphant. The grimacing, upturned faces, about to disintegrate into laughter, were telling him that a horse's yud wasn't really round, but shaped by nose, ears and teeth. Clearly, a horse did not have a *circular* head.

'Well. We'da all know the old and true saying. Cleanliness is next to Godliness. And I make mention of the beautiful hoss, yea, as the cleanest animal putt upon God's beautiful earth. I wouldn't be afeared of eating after a hoss. It is *assuredly* so.' Everyone could now relax, and the threatened, awful embarrassment of only half-stifled giggles did not further deflect Emmanuel from his adventuresome oratory.

On yet another occasion, however, he was unable to stave off this, the worst of all calamities. While reaching up on tiptoe, lunging out his arms to make a particularly dramatic point, the margarine box at last gave way with a splintering, blasphemous crack, and Emmanuel fell into ignominy, below the level of the pulpit. A moment's horrified pause, and his head appeared once more in view, shakily above fingers clutching at the dark oak.

'Be not afeared!' he announced with great dignity, 'for tis I.'

Such things are but fragments, amusing sidelines, of the local chapel tradition. I do not want you to laugh with malice: writing about Salem now, in London, as the District Line clatters through less than a hundred yards away, I find it difficult to recall any one particular physical impression – certainly, I remember the clean but contained smell of the place, like water from a fresh pot of flowers, but mostly I get the confusing impressions of that strange feeling of satisfaction chapel provokes. A feeling which need have little or perhaps even nothing to do with religion. My own personal feelings on *that* subject have nothing to do with this chapter, and are too confused, anyway, to be written about in an interesting or relevant manner, but it does not take a religious man (which I certainly am not) to write in praise of the chapels. This probably makes it easier for me to recognize that Salem, Zion, and scores of similar institutions cannot be easily chipped away from the greater bulk of the life which used to exist in the Forest of Dean, and which still inserts itself into the language and styles of the present. These chapels, standing firm in the centres of the villages, ugly and immovable, call forth to the sound of their own windily insistent music the meetings, the play of words, the charabanc outings to the Malverns or the seaside, the reputations of a good many public speakers, the former attendance of, at one time or another, almost everyone in the district; with the miners singing their yearning hymns through the dark, wet wood on the way home from work, the sound of 'Bread of Heaven' in the pubs and, most of all, with the formulation and the nourishment of at least a *kind* of hope and a social consciousness. Again, I repeat, it does not take a religious man to write in praise of the chapels, but maybe one needs to be a bit of a political evangelist.

There *is* a little sadness in such a fall, surely, and a degree of futile melancholy in the over-hearty singing of those who are left, and a necessity for a gratitude which is far from quaint or sentimental. But the chapels are not finished yet, and occasionally make a passing show not only of survival, but even of growth. I hear of another outing to Weston-super-Mare or Barry Island, another improvement to another building, another appeal to the ebbing but still sizeable sentiment of the local people, which almost, but never quite works.

And at Harvest Festival – even the pubs have their harvest festivals, though the club, as part of its steady drifting change, gave up theirs last year – and especially on Anniversary Day, where the children sing and recite three times in one day, the chapel becomes, once again, the full image of its older days. But there is a touch of hard-working deliberation about such a resurrection. At this Anniversary Time, crinkling with new dresses, the three local chapels, Salem and Zion in Berry Hill, and Joyford chapel at the bottom of Joyford Hill, half a mile down an extremely steep and coiled slope, held their services on consecutive Sundays so that people could, at one of the three long services held in the day, on at least one of the three Sundays in the summer, have no excuse for missing them. Joyford Chapel has now been locked up, and the two houses nearest to it have also been abandoned. Since this small village deep under the hill is off the bus routes, far from work, and a steep walk away from most other signs of activity in the more up-to-date sense, there has been a gradual move away from the place. It is no longer thought to be quite such a good village in which to live, particularly by the younger people.

Thus, first the older institutions and pursuits, and then the most out-of-the-way places themselves begin to fall into decay.

The bus services to Gloucester have had to be extended, and now more than two thousand people travel daily to the city in order to work. Movement is *away* all the time, and the pull of the industrial midlands has also had its effect. Those who work in Gloucester and beyond, travelling by bus more than twenty miles each way, leave earlier, get home hours later than they used to, finding themselves far less wrapped up in the life of such a small unit as their village. A Cinderford bus company advertises tours to the continent, and people get out on a Sunday in their cars, and I'm glad for them. 'Sunday School anniversary services at Salem Free Church on Whit Sunday were well attended,' reports the *Dean Forest Guardian* of May 26, 1961. 'At 11 a.m. Mr H. E. Harris was chairman, and in the afternoon Miss Margaret Gwilliam, Head Mistress of English Bicknor School, conducted the service. The annual Sunday School outing took place on Whit Monday, when Porthcawl was visited.'

Those few people on the normal Sunday at Salem and Zion do not fully realize, I suspect, why they are so few and why their numbers will not grow, no matter how hard they pray.

SIX

After I had been to Salem (for the first time in a good many years) I walked the fifty or so yards across the main road to 'The Globe', trying to avoid the many puddles with their thin coatings of mottled and dirty ice. In winter time the Forest villages, usually perched upon or just below the crown of a hill, have a marooned and grey-stone-cold, harsh appearance, as if holding on out of the most miserable kind of habit. You are made always to be very much aware of the weather and the seasons in a place like this, where rain slants so easily and so frequently and the wind launches itself through the trees and clefts in the hills. Now, red-nosed and bad tempered with feeling so numb, I cursed the place: at the top of the council-house climb I could see a few men leaning into the wind, hands disappeared and a dog was walking sideways. At 'The Globe', my favourite pub, the fireplace was piled high with huge, blazing lumps of local coal, and the early arrivals were smacking their hands over it, talking in low, cold voices. Some of them had come through the lanes or across 'the meand', or even through the wood, now a huge soft cathedral of cold. The Forest is beautiful at this time in a different, more aloof fashion than when green with summer, and the feel of the place becomes more immediately apparent. I suppose one feels a return to the sense of isolation and severely separated villages, that, too, there is something unbearably evocative about the stamping of feet outside the blazing windows and the bustle of coats, hats, greetings which follows.

My father was in 'The Globe', with a pint of cider, and we went and sat down together as near to the fire as possible. I blew on my hands.

'It's cold in the chapel,' I said a bit self-righteously.

'You've bin to chapel then?' My father seemed pleased. It would have produced the same contentment if I had said I had gone to band practice or to a meting of the rugby club committee.

'Yes. There weren't many there though – less than a dozen. Not many at all.'

'Not many there?' Dad sounded incredulous, and disappointed. Most of the others in the room would have shown the same momentary reaction, jolted back to a surprise which reflected a former pattern but not the present village life. It was as if returning from a long holiday and hearing that the Wolves were in the Fourth Division or that Cardiff first fifteen had failed to win a match all season. I have noticed before, in other circumstances, that people are liable to act as though they believed the climate or assumptions of a previous existence continue to run parallel with the present of which they are a part, ready to break through and cause those moments of startled recognition that things have, after all, changed considerably. But in the Forest, in particular, I think that very few of the older generation will face up to the full picture of change as it has unrolled over the last decade in these villages and little towns, even though they may be beneficiaries or accomplices of the agencies creating such change. They don't want to know about it, so that the often-heard regrets come into being unlocked together, as isolated irritations about specific examples rather than as a general elegy for the Forest of Dean they used to know. And yet, despite their acceptance of the new, together with such a cloak of evasions and withdrawals, their language remains much the same, giving one at times the stranger (and grossly exaggerated) impression of a whole generation acting in some carefully and elaborately conspired ritual, speaking lines which no longer have their original relevance but are not yet ready to be forgotten. The younger Foresters, it will seem in turn, have come to be contemptuous of such meticulously performed delusions for they know the words off by heart, in angry rote.

Outside 'The Globe', a couple of cars had coughed to a halt on the icy patch of waste ground nearest the road and the telephone box. The days when a car, or a privately owned house, would have been a legitimate occasion for hostile comment have long since gone the way to quaintness, and the vague tinges of iniquity have also faded away from most other signs of individual wealth and large-scale personal property. Enmity is now more likely to be directed at the trappings rather than the material substance of middle-class life: accent, mannerism and so on. The class consciousness of the older Foresters exists still, but in a less uncompromising form, but many of the younger inhabitants I questioned (or, rather, spoke to) used 'class' without such a colouring when the concept was accepted at all – 'better class' meant approval for nicer things, like upholstered seats in a lounge bar or steak instead of fish-and-chips, rather than things necessarily denied them because of their job or even their education. For both groups, a gentler world has arrived, where almost all of the old social and political invective has been toned down, and where personal ambition, whether for possessions or higher social status, has become, if still not entirely 'respectable', at least a common possibility.

The domestic styles of brighter fashions, clearer, neater wallpaper and flimsily 'elegant' modern furniture seem to be related to the softer, more restrained and more tolerant system of personal habits. It would, of course, still be unthinkable to be a homosexual or an adulterer in the village, and wearing dirty clothes on a Sunday remains a bit suspect. Gossip can be cruel here, and has the horrible weight of generations of chapel language behind it. I have seen examples of a really terrible intolerance on too many occasions to feel too glib about the values in working-class culture, even though I certainly believe in them as they can and ought to extend and develop. (The reader will, I hope, excuse such comments: it is better if my attitudes emerge out of description. The temptations of the shrill voice are very strong for me, but in writing about the Forest of Dean, I feel a *little* more humble than usual.)

'The Globe' itself, always an extremely popular Berry Hill centre (and still the place for the band and rugby players to gather after practice or a game), has changed almost as much as the Club. I think, though, that the public places changed after the living rooms, after the front-room revolutions, yet this seems to be the other way round in many other places in

Britain. The main room of 'The Globe' used to be entirely masculine and functional, admitting that the hard business of drinking needed few frills and little signs of quiet, feminine domestication. However, there was a pair of antlers at the top of the room, and lots of pictures of former rugby teams squatting before their cups, and concert parties leering back at the camera. These remain, a trifle out of place. But the long tables and split benches have been put away or chopped up, and now there are little tables with individual chairs, scattered around, giving the place – in comparison to its former appearance – a café-like look. Similarly, at an old, rather drab pub at Mile End, another of the outlying Coleford villages, the Yorkshire-born landlord has schemes for a saloon bar, an indoor ladies' lavatory and 'a better class of trade, as there isn't a decent pub in the whole Forest of Dean'. He keeps a gleaming Jaguar outside the low stone walls in the front of the pub.

The atmosphere in 'The Globe' remains much the same, however. There has been no great change in the customers – perhaps a few more wives, a coloured shirt or two; a few less caps and 'best' trilbys. It's still not a place for suede boots, silk cravats and the growing number of local dandies. Strangers are looked at, and discussed, with the same faintly conspiratorial air; the talk is broad Forest, as strong in memory as the cutting vinegar-sharp smell of cider or the sticky, richer odour of draught beer.

'How bist, Will,' grunted one of the middle-aged men by the window as a pale-faced, slightly furtive-looking man went to the table for his pint, 'nice and warm enough?'

'Oy.'

Nearly everyone had managed to find out that Will and

his wife had had a quarrel that morning, and that Will had come off worst.

'Everything alright at home?' The questioner was about to overstep a firm rule. Will half-turned towards him, pursing his rubbery little mouth.

'Oy,' he said. Then, as a minor concession, 'alright. But better now I got a pint, though.' The other laughed, suitably put in his place.

Your business is known, your troubles are known, your family is known, your weaknesses are known. Conversation here, in this pub, as in the other old-style local places, is rarely impersonal. It is wise not to break too many rules, not to be too selfish or uppety. This feeling of closeness, and of familiarity and a sense of family, is still there, for it is not in such places as these that you will find them as splintered as elsewhere in the village and in the Forest as a whole. The tougher elements of the local young men will go here rather than to some of the newer, smarter places. Here, too, you will find the middle-aged miner, or ex-miner, cutting away from the demands of home, and the remaining people who contrive to go out every night that they have money. Yet these are becoming increasingly less typical. Who, then, are the people who stay at home, or do not go often to 'The Globe' or the Club, who do not watch the rugby team or ask after the score, who are not interested in the band and have forgotten all about the chapel, who do not work in the pit and who use the distinct Forest words only when they are not thinking about it, or when other people are not looking? Do they stay at home to dig their gardens?

I know them, of course, but they are less easy to describe. A new life has been swelling up beneath the traditional

66

framework of Forest life. For the first time there are faces in the village to which you cannot immediately put a name and a history. Who, I wondered (perhaps a bit patronizingly), buys the Danish blue cheese they sell at the shop?

Truthfully, there were plaster flying ducks in descending order of size across the living-room wall, which itself was painted, I was told, in Brolac Plastic Emulsion Paint, lime green. It was a nice, gentle colour. The mirror on the wall opposite the flat window was oval, and webbed with gilt. The deep armchairs stood on little black legs, and the centre of the room was uncluttered, showing the large smudge-like contemporary-style carpet. I put down a cup of Nescafé on to a little table with wheels, sat back, and found a slight tremble at the backs of my legs.

'Have a bit more cake?' It was put on to a fresh plate, and I broke the cake with my fingers.

I don't know why I feel so ill at ease. They were friendly, and I knew them. It was a relief that we should be getting the new things, the washing machines, vacuum cleaners and carpets. I feel like punching in the eye those who talk about 'the new paternalism' when the New Left talks about affluence. When I was born, my father was on two shifts a week, and it took a World War to change that. Now that my mother has a washing machine *and* a refrigerator you will not find us talking about a threatened dignity or a lost nobility!

Why, then, these stirrings of discomfort, in this house, and that house, in the circle of new council houses at the top of the village? I must try to answer, and describe. This was the village in another way, growing far beyond the one I had grown up into. I had the impression that I was not the only

67

one who was slightly uncomfortable, slightly puzzled. This was a newer, less tangible kind of anxiety – not an anxiety about work, or lack of food, or growing old, but about how to live, what to get, what was right and what was not suitable.

'I see that you take the *Daily Telegraph*, then?'

'Yes,' and with a slight laugh. After a momentary pause, the husband, who worked in an office now (and had once worked in the pit) thought that an explanation was needed. (I swear I did not ask the question in a hostile or impertinent way.) 'We used to take the *Herald*. Our dad used to have the *Worker* – and I didn't think I'd ever read this. But they all do on the bus – anyway, a good many of them do.' Another pause. 'There's lots of rugby news in it, you know.' I agreed. 'It's not a bad paper, really. You get the other side – and it's not all so simple as we once used to make out, is it? Besides, they all take the *Telegraph* in the office, except some of the girls. I suppose I didn't feel all that comfortable not being the same, what with being a bit like a fish out of water to start with, and so on.'

I liked him very much, and admired his courage in making a change. He would not have been able to do it ten years ago, for he would have felt the power of some old taboo, the almost indefinable but nagging sense of backsliding associated with this new and cleaner kind of work.

'Do you ever go to the Club now?' I asked, later. (I was not only asking questions, of course, and I was not listening-to-make-notes. This conversation, incorporating parts of another, cannot possibly be recognized by the person concerned in the very unlikely event of his reading this book.)

'No, not much. I get a bit bored with it, to tell you the truth. There's better things to do with my time. . . .'

'The band is alright in its way. I think I should be sorry to see it go. But that's about all. I like to hear them at Christmas, mind.'

'I haven't given a thought to chapel in years. . . .'

'I used to roll my own. Then it took up too much time and all that.' He laughed in self-parody. 'Anyway, this is today's cigarette.' I was smoking them too, and very rarely roll my own. Many of the jingle-jangle phrases of current advertising keep slipping into popular speech, and I even saw two little boys going down the road saying a commercial as they kicked a can from one to the other, just as earlier children would sing, half-understandingly about some popular entertainer. 'I like to keep an open mind – they're all up to the same game,' is what, with similar variations, I have heard replacing the former combative language about politics. There was the realization, I think, that there were many other things which could be packaged and sold like a branded product.

I notice that one of the coach firms in Cinderford advertises 'family tours' of the continent, and very many in the Forest do now travel abroad. Yet quite a few of the older women have not been to London, and are incapable of imagining what it is like, except as a bigger and smokier and dirtier-as-well-as-brighter Gloucester. I noticed, too, that almost every household I knew or visited took women's magazines, though they were still called 'books'. The old, more specifically 'working-class' *Red Letter* and *The Oracle* have given way to the brighter, more indeterminate weeklies and monthlies. The Club does not take the *Daily*

Worker any longer, which I think is a pity. There is still not an adequate library service (in my opinion) or a good bookshop (this is beyond dispute) in the Forest. The local amateur dramatic societies put on farces and weary stock plays with comic butlers and maids, or an occasional light musical, and there is no legitimate theatre in Gloucester. I met very few people who regretted these things, and yet very many who were pleased or relieved that the older culture of the area was on the retreat: all that seems to be replacing it is a greater privacy, a more anxious assessment of oneself and one's neighbour ('How Do Your Neighbours Rate You,' begins an advertisement in the local paper – a national advertisement, it is fair to add, for a local branch), and a greater sense of *potential* rather than actual mobility. Where it was once thought rather amusing and cissy to go to the grammar school, now this is an occasion for great worry, a relief or disappointment as the results may go.

Since fewer and fewer men are going to work in the local pits, there is less shift work, so that the villages seem emptier in the day. Formerly, groups of men would meet on the corner, at the pub, or go walking – dull enough, it would seem, but part of that collective exchange of gossip and opinion which plays so large a part in working-class life. Now, more often, they have been split up – the people waiting at the bus stop after tea are off to the cinema or to a dance. Local firms line up with dinner dances at places like Chepstow, and there is less and less an obvious common meeting ground – it's not at the chapel, at the rugby ground, at the band room or on the corner, and there's nowhere else where it could be at present. Increasingly, the pubs are being segregated according to comfort and the type of person likely to be there – young men in Berry Hill, for instance, will travel a long way to find the right sort of pub with the right sort of chairs and the right sort of conversation. There is a turning away, or a turning of backs.

And at the same time, there is a turning towards something better, something we would all choose. It is only that, in the process, the possibilities and splendour always held within the older, tighter environs have been or are being denied. 'Community' will soon be a thing to plan for, as if this were a Surrey town or a place being built up from scratch.

Sitting in 'The Globe', on the other side of my father, was Teddy Gwilliam, a man who holds himself like a young officer in the Guards, for all that he has a large family and, unlike such young gentlemen, works on his knees in one of the small, licensed pits which are another characteristic of the Forest of Dean, still thriving like tiny piglets round the great black half-dead sows of the bigger mines. He works it with his two brothers, and they live by what coal can be got out, which sometimes, when picking through earth and rock, or when a promising seam peters out, can be nothing at all for days or even weeks on end, but at other times is good enough or promising enough to allow a longer break for 'bread' and more of a chat in the little wooden hut they have erected near the black cavity in the earth which slants into the slope of a tree-covered hill.

Teddy has a natural, impressive dignity which deserves better than my comparison with a Guards officer, for his bearing is quiet, helped no doubt by a high, well-shaped forehead from which his hair has retreated. He talks rather in

71

a monotone, but one is rarely likely to be bored by it because he is one of those rare individuals for whom almost everything has some sudden and special interest, some unusual angle. He might almost have come from a George Eliot novel: most of all, he is continually fascinated by the skills and the peculiarities of his job, which he appears to regard as a privilege rather than a burden – to be cussed at, of course, and be disappointed in too many times, but all the same a privilege and a freedom, a regular and complete means of expression. As a consequence, his attitude to his work, the attitude of a proud and almost self-sufficient craftsman, is anachronistic to modern ears. (The sense in which it could be said 'We are all workers now' is only possible if we are all shysters now.)

The small mines of the Forest, employing two, four or even a dozen men, have been part of the local landscape for centuries, racking houses, killing workers and depositing little mole-like tumps with extravagant frequency. They would really need a book on their own to be understood properly, existing by a combination of 'ancient privilege' and the type of land and land-ownership found in the area. Their names have a strange ring about them, like New Fancy or Ready Penny, and in the past but much less so today, they were important in local life, rarely producing great wealth, yet emphasizing the values of independence and village identity. (It will not escape the reader's attention, I suppose, that I have difficulty in describing or explaining these qualities, for you cannot build a jig-saw by describing its pieces.)

These small pits are subject to inspection and national safety regulations, but in other ways remain 'private' – very much at the small workshop stage of the industrial revolution, rather as the ownership of land in the Forest, which belongs mainly to the Crown, remains at an even earlier stage. The pit worked by the Gwilliam brothers – one tall and dignified, one stocky and ebullient, a good rugby player, and the other shy and impressively strong – is at Braceland, half a mile from Berry Hill and Ninewells. It has the cinematic appearance of a small prospector's camp in the Rocky Mountains, for the working area is swallowed up in the trees, some of which have sagged wearily towards each other as a result of the steady eating away of rock and soil down beneath their roots. The land is unsteady here, with small gradients working against the slope, and a long stony fall to the Wye a mile to the west. Two tub-wide tunnels are driven into the bank, ultimately connecting with each other as they creep into the darkness: there is, therefore, an escape route and a freer flow of air. A small thread of railway emerges from each to converge again on a pile of damp, messy-looking rubble which turns out to be small coal. There was mud everywhere, of a rich, oozy, squelchy kind. Props of timber and neat stacks of chunky logs lay in the foreground, an axe was stuck into a bigger log, and a cloud of almost pure white wood smoke hung in the drooping branches of the tree which acts as a second roof above the small timber shack the brothers use as office, planning centre, eating place and cloakroom.

In the shack, which is placed on one of the few bits of level ground, a platform above the valley, they keep a small trunk which has a carefully rolled, pen-drawn map, neatly shaded to show what coal they might expect to find on this site. From the map, it is clear that the area has been worked

73

before, and Ted told me he was going back to what his father had left years ago.

'I'm after what fayther left long before the war.'

It was in winter when I first scraped up the tunnel to the place where the brothers were grunting with each chink of their tools, biting into the dark vein which seeps out of the earth and rock like a slow, faint stain. I would not have recognized it as coal, imprisoned in the sides of the face. Ted shadowed up before me like a bent wizard in a magic lantern show, and there was a faint trickle of water.

'Nervous?' Ted asked, certain in his mind that I was. I was.

'No,' I said, for reasons of pride, 'it's rather cosy up in here, en it?'

My back was already wet, and aching with the effort of keeping bent. I was also once kicked rather savagely in the knee when playing rugby for Berry Hill against another Forest of Dean side – an entirely predictable injury, but not less painful – and it hurts when I keep it bent for very long. After twenty minutes, let alone a full day every day, I was an old crock, and soon wanted to creep back to the opening and the light. But, with a genuinely captive listener, Teddy kept talking, the steady, quiet rhythm of his speech mounting every now and then to enthusiasm as he described what he was about, or softening into a slightly amused concern as I grunted and shifted uncomfortably, holding on to the clammy, cold wall of the tunnel.

'Look,' my captor was explaining, a strange note in his voice, 'you can see here where the old men have been.' He pointed to some rough, barely discernible lines in the rock to one side of him, his body stretching forward to the limits of stability while still balanced on the one knee. The marks looked as though they had been made by a frightened cat trying to claw its way back to safety.

'What old men?'

'Oh, years and years back, o'but. Most of this land here has been gone over and gone over till there yunt all that much coal for we poor lot to get out, I can tell tha.' Teddy laughed with admiration for the old Foresters, and with more wonder than regret. ' 'Sknow what? I should like to go back, just once, just for a bit, and see how they managed. They must have been marvellous people, Den.' He shifted. 'Oy, they must have bin. They didn't have the same tools as we had, mind – practically no metal. We found an old wooden spade down here – oy, it makes you wonder, it do.' He was silent again.

Soon, they were back at work, the three of them, talking finished for a while. Each of the brothers specialized in a different aspect of the job, one feeding the coal back to the other in a steady, crumbly mount, and the third bringing in the timber or pulling out the fat, heavy iron tubs, trundling with a slow clatter along the small line curving out from the tunnel. Their cap lamps glowed and fluttered in the dark, approached and retreated, blacked out and then flared up again, and the tunnel edged its way pickshaft lengths deeper into the hill, further below the tree roots and the rotting layers of dead winter leaves.

Afterwards, in the hut, the early gloom already overtaking and filling in the surrounding woods, showing up boldly the yellow square of light from the only house that could be seen, a few hundred yards below the present levels, the brothers talked about their work and their leisure. They were very impressive, sure of what they were doing and why they were doing it. I cannot think that there will be many others like them from my generation in the Forest of Dean.

'No, I couldn't work in a factory,' Teddy was as emphatic as it is possible to be, 'I couldn't abear it. Clocking in and clocking out. Never in control of what you'd want to do, always at somebody or other's beck and call.' Harold and Dennis, his brothers, agreed, and explained the virtues of being craftsmen working to their own pace and their own needs, cruelly hard on some days when a piece of ground was difficult, but more relaxed on others when the coal was coming out in easier fashion. 'Nobody publishes our absentee figures, or sends away a little card to some big office.' They were acutely conscious of the silly hierarchies they would have to encounter in the local factories, and intended to avoid the mentality behind the terminology of 'staff' and 'workers' so disliked by the miners from the big pits when they had changed their jobs. They didn't mind the hard or dirty work of a factory, if that is what it was, but they rejected the things which went with it.

Ted was not greatly impressed with many of the changes which have made their onslaught on the Forest of Dean, precisely because they involved some challenge to his individuality and his dignity. Let the coloured balloons float down on the ballroom dancers, he said, 'We shan't have a works dinner!' His life, his work and his values, like those of his brothers, remained unchanged, convincing himself (and me) that he had managed to hold on to some quality the rest might have let slip.

As elsewhere, of course, there is an uneasy relationship between the new and the stubborn but virtually doomed habits of the old. Unfortunately, we tend to see only the perversity or the quaintness of the latter, neglecting everything but the obvious incongruity. The Gwilliam brothers, and some few others of their kind in the Forest of Dean, act and think as though their labour was the most essential part of their personality, owed to themselves and not marketable by the demands of others, using it as a defence as well as an expression. 'Independence' is a popular claim in the Forest, but it is a rather meaningless concept when applied to the life of a working man, or to almost any of us; Teddy Gwilliam used the word, in a valid but retreating sense, to mean freedom from the irksome evasions of the capital-labour relationship which is inevitably seen in the life and spirit of the local factories; freedom from their hierarchies and their power. Perhaps it is too much to ask of the world, but meanwhile, there is the damp, curving tunnel and the mounds of small coal, the work of a lifetime.

SEVEN

'CLIFF.'

The name was chalked on the wall with juvenile earnestness. A name to be mouthed with ecstasy. The name of a pleasant enough young pop singer.

But what was it doing here, on this wall, in the Forest of Dean? Might not one have expected something like 'May Day for Peace' or 'Keep the Pits Open'? Actually, in 1961, one would not, of course. Somehow, and with immense, sprawling complexity, the life that goes on, the personal and social relationships which are always there, as well as the new developing habits, are of a piece, easier to satirize than comprehend: the neon-dressed pop singer jerking over the echo-chambered microphone as if in orgasm is most popular in the long grey streets of back-to-back houses, and here, in the Forest, the splendid old man with the polished watch chain, who knows Genesis off by heart, likes 'Wagon Train' and 'Double Your Money'.

'CLIFF.' Yes, indeed. But a young person is bound to

have put it there, just as young people's money has created him.

'I think he's marvellous,' tapped the young, podgy-faced girl, vivid and alarming in a tangerine-tight and tangeriney-coloured sweater. She also wore a long, drooping row of thick, mottled beads. We were at the same table in the most recent of the two juke-box cafés in Coleford. What is more, she had actually *touched* Cliff 'in person'.

'Well, what do you think of this place – the Forest, I mean?'

'This *dump* you mean.'

'I don't know,' I hedged, 'I don't think it's all that bad. I'll bet you'd like to come back if you moved away. What's so bad about it?' She intended to tell me anyway, for although we did not know each other, we had laughed when I had accidentally made a disgusting blurbing noise while sucking up the last of the cola.

'It's just half dead, that's what. And lots of mopey old people. Nothing to do. Lot of bloody old miseries round here – they've had their day!'

I mentioned a few things that one could do, but didn't say that the scenery was very nice.

'The coffee bars and that are alright – but there yunt enough of them, is there? And I will say as its pretty round here. But you can't look at pictures all day.'

As the conversation developed, in fits and starts due to a mutual shyness (I also thought, to my shame, what if some of the more gossipy Berry Hill lot see me in here buying a soft drink for a sexy-looking female, and me a married man: this kind of caution is very much a necessity still in the Forest) it became clear that she still looked upon 'being a Forester' as something unusual and, in its way, privileged. This feeling, at least, persists.

Young Foresters, consequently, have both more than the conventional regard and yet more than the conventional hostility for the place of their birth. They are the pop generation but they are also the inheritors of a long local tradition, so that the tensions are worked out in terms of family, and especially in the ways apparently conflicting chunks of old and new Forest culture are joined in their persons. A youth can belong to the village band as 'something to do', look upon it with a certain amused condescension, and yet be affected by it and feel himself linked to the old photographs in the Y.M.C.A. building at Berry Hill. He will argue at home, and then, outside, defend from the opposite point of view: this is what rapid change means in a small locality, and this is also why surface descriptions of 'change' seem so often to be caricature.

Inevitably the younger Foresters have discovered or have been induced to 'discover' very different interests and ways of spending their time. There is, importantly, a greater freedom about sex, although not by any means a startling change – it's just that conversation about it is possible in mixed company, that the old-style obscenities of excess prudery have been abandoned. And there are probably a few less of the small-town-style part-time harlots. Dress is certainly more colourful, more urgently a matter of fashion, and small stores like Cullis' of Mile End have become as sophisticated as any shop of comparable size in, say, Balham or Balsall Heath. Economically, the sons and daughters of those used to scrimping and scraping and bread and dripping dinners, are wealthy: the biggest aspiration is to get a car, and the Forest roads are no longer so rural in appearance when they approach the main clusters of villages. One of the biggest changes in the life of the district lies for all to see in the shop windows, and in the number of new television and electrical goods shops, the new shop-fittings, the frozen-food counters, the record shops and the new garages. In Berry Hill, the fish and chip shop has closed down, but they are selling second-hand cars at the garage.

'Like hot cakes, butty,' said Alan Lodge, 'hot cakes in the temple.' A suitably enigmatic remark.

The young Conservative groups in the Forest of Dean are (it would have once been impossible to believe) extremely successful, and many of their members come from working-class families. They hold 'out-door barbecues' and deliberately gay functions, with a zest that is sadly lacking in the Socialist equivalent. I am a friend of a few who belong to the Coleford branch, and I think I know and, in part, understand why they should do this (on the face of it) pretty obnoxious thing. After all, it is one of the more clearly unpleasant organizations of the political scene – when politics enter into it – and only a high degree of political illiteracy would allow the sons and daughters of coalminers to wear its badge. But, invective apart, wear it they do.

Some of these strange members have made a deliberate choice, and one which at times I can scarce forbear to cheer myself. They have rejected what they take to be 'the past' and stomped eagerly and loudly into their conception of the future. They are not more callous or less sensitive than the rest of us, but have opted for that which seems most like personal emancipation.

'The more you get on,' I was told by someone who had

been to primary school with me, 'the more like a real person you get. You're less tied – less to your parents and to the Forest and all that goes with it. You've found that yourself, haven't you?'

There is, of course, a huge amount of truth in that, but 'individual' is a loaded word in this or any similar context. Understandably, for many of my generation and younger in the Forest of Dean, the extraordinary power and subtlety of the old culture has threatened us too darkly, clouding the jingle of 'outside' and 'getting on'. As a result, anything which is collective in the old ways, that smacks of ponderous and too-nostalgic talk on the themes of 'a sense of community', is associated with the drab and the second-rate. 'Complete stock of food FREE with every refrigerator,' 'How to buy shares that MUST go up,' say two advertisements in an issue of the local paper, and the same edition carries a headline 'Lydney Youths Ripped Bubble Gum Machine Off Wall.' 'Community', in contrast, is coming to mean old women with knitting needles gossiping in tin huts, where the rain makes a thundering noise on the roof. And if the older Foresters believe, as some of them do, that the new generations have lost the cohesion of 'warmth' or purpose that was once characteristic of the place, they should remember that the younger people are unable to discover what they mean, in any but the most banal and accidental of senses. Service to the club, the union, the local government committees, the band, chapel, football team, choir and so on is, of course, no longer the same, and talk of 'the executive of the Union' or 'the wardens of the chapel' has an element of parody about it in present circumstances.

The pace is now set by other agencies, as a few simple

contrasts drawn out of the area will soon show: the Youth Club and the Welfare Clinic at Berry Hill are both held in what is called 'the hut' by everyone in the village, a Y.M.C.A. building with creaking boards and an old stove. A record player provides the zip for the former, and a row of prams indicate the change of function – and there are, of course, many other local activities held within the building. (I remember as a child being enormously impressed and bewildered by a version of *Wuthering Heights* put on by a touring 'ham' company.) The rugby club has hardly enough money to survive. There are few adequate halls for amateur dramatic societies, music clubs or even the brass bands. The Trade Unions are not involved in anything that could remotely seem exciting and down-to-earth. Welfare services for the old are very inadequate. Some of the older schools rise up like old prints in the history of public education, with shabby classrooms, smelly out-buildings and underpaid teachers. The public authorities, the God-like nationalizers, have closed the pits and the local railway passenger lines, and the remaining public transport meets with general abuse. It is a familiar and depressing list, which might easily be lengthened: the list of all that is 'public' and 'communal'.

Now, turn to the other side. The factory in Coleford is part of the giant Beecham group, publishes a chatty works magazine, gives its workers an annual bonus according to their salary and years of service, and has shown, with other local factories, some of the ability to make loyalty to the company above loyalty to the union or to workers in other industries. 'Welfare' provided by the private companies in terms of pensions, staff benefit schemes, social facilities and so on appears to extend far in range and imagination – almost completely removing the firmly outlined spectres behind the old talk of 'them' and 'us' in work terms, although not completely so. And, always and for ever, as the pop language has it, another set of values or other and brighter means of enjoyment create an impossible contrast to the old Forest. There are so many differences between the generations now (with advantages on both sides) that it would take more than a montage of conversations to illustrate them. Some cruelties are no longer possible, and some hopes are no longer 'possible'.

For instance (and how pointless I feel it is to say 'for instance', but perhaps something in these examples will gel) I remember an old deaf woman, whom I'll call Mrs Baker, who lived on the lower slopes of the village and who had a hole in the back wall of her house that had been stuffed up with sacking.

'Good morning, Mrs Baker,' a neighbour would say, walking to the shop, simpering at her with absolute friendliness, 'good morning, you silly old bugger.'

'Good morning, Doris,' the old woman would reply, aware that she had been greeted, but not hearing the words.

'Wiped your arse this morning?' and Mrs Baker would smile, and nod her head, and smile. It was thought to be wildly amusing by some of the village women. It was, in any case, not untypical of some of the humour and unthinking callousness of a few in the district.

Or again, the collections for those injured or out of work, the concerts, the giving and taking, the warmth of familiarity and a kind of trust. Even in the deplorable happening above, although that would be hard to believe. The dinners keeping hot under a plate taken to the old man living alone, the flow of a common vocabulary – all these things which might sound romantic if I did not know them to be true, and had not experienced the tide of it myself.

'It's no use, Dennis,' pointed out an acquaintance, 'no matter how much you go on about it, but I can't, I just *can't* talk to our old mon – Him do sit there grumbling about the cost of this or the cost of that, kipping his money in a *purse* – then we'da hear about what they did when they were on short time, or what Cooke said at Speech House, when the tree was struck by lightning. I don't want to hear about it – it's nothing to do with me, is it?'

'No, no,' another said, elsewhere, 'the trouble with young people like you is that you think you'll always get things pushed on a plate in front of you. Go on, admit it. It won't last, I tell you, it *bloody well can't last!*'

'We spent nearly sixty quid on our holiday.'

'Mr Evans reminded the audience that the present generation were picking the rich fruits from the tree which would not have grown had not the older miners cultivated the land beneath it so well – there was a need for the principles of unionism to be stamped on the hearts of the younger people and on the present generation of workers' (report in *Dean Forest Guardian*).

'Legs-eleven,' Brian Harris called, 'No. 10 – Macmillan's Den. Clickity-click-sixty-six.'

'House!' a voice shouted. 'That'll pay for what I've lost on thik fruit machine.' This, in the working men's club.

'Many here remember when there was no ambulance at hand to take an injured man home; when there was no first-aid kit in the pit to dress the wounds of an injured man. The present generation of miners know very little about strikes; there were many local strikes in our day. We went through three bitter national strikes – 1912, when we asked for a minimum wage, locked out for eleven weeks in 1921 and we went on strike for seven months in 1926: in that strike some of our best trade unionists never had a day's work in the pit again.' (*Dean Forest Guardian*)

'I like that Hughie Green on the telly,' a faded woman in a flowered apron almost smacked her hands together, 'he's so sincere.'

'They're good – those commercials. Some of them, anyway.'

'AS ADVERTISED ON YOUR TELEVISION.' 'AS SEEN ON YOUR SCREEN.'

'Holidays with pay was just a dream in our time. Most Forest miners never had a holiday in their lives away from home. The young people of today may look on us as a bunch of squares, but the truth is that we in our day fought hard and long to get the rich things which the young people of today are enjoying. It seems to me absurb that a sexy doll who moans and wails a sloppy song can get £50 or £100 for one performance yet the old age pensioner gets a meagre £2 10s. a week, and lives a week on the price of a shirt. It is a national disgrace that those who, by their labour, brought the economy of this country to its present level are now virtually a forgotten people. But for coal and the collier, this country would have been a fifth-rate country.' (*Dean Forest Guardian*)

'I don't know how my mum stuck it. She had to drag in the bath, keep polishing the hob, never go out. We never thought when *we* got married that we'd have a car. We don't know we're born today.'

'We should have gone right on in there,' said the young miner about Suez, 'but this country is not capable of it any more. Not even against the bloody wogs.'

But amongst the older Foresters there is a refusal to accept not only that 'them' are not exactly the same (and, indeed, they might well be), but also that Great Britain is not as powerful as she always was. 'It's the hard work of people like us what made this country what it is today,' claimed one of the speechmakers, and this country is the envy of the entire world, the greatest there has ever been. An imperial idea lingers, confusingly, with the fundamentalist and puritanical socialism.

'Let the Russians just start something, that's all,' a close relative told me, in one of his rare belligerent moods, after we had both been drinking cider-and-ruby wine, 'and then they'll have *us* to face. Like Hitler did – oy, and the bloody Kaiser. And there yunt an army in the world as ool touch the British army, you mark my words.'

'What about the Americans? I should think they'd be the most important lot if—'

'The Americans? The Yanks?' incredulity overtook bewilderment. What the hell had the Americans got to do with it? Lot of crepe-soled softies with gum and girls.

My father loathes uniforms and talk of war in the newspapers, but cannot believe that we have made ourselves dependent on the United States, or so second-rate in terms of power politics. The maps in the dripping, peeling classrooms had been red with 'our property' (this was how it was explained to me, as well as to my father, by a splendidly fierce and energetic old woman, brandishing her pointer as though it was the instrument of conquest itself) and, in unemployment and lock-out, poor pay and bad housing, much of the talk, a lot of the handed-down pomp and pretensions, the marching of the bands, echoed the style and certainties of the insular arrogance and ritualized grandeur of the idea of Empire.

In some of the older cottages of the Forest of Dean (for instance in a row of houses on the Ruspidge road coming from Cinderford, in East Dean), along with the heavy dressers stacked high with ornately designed but usually chipped crockery, the brown doors and window-sills and flowered wallpaper and thick-legged chairs, you will now and then find pictures of greyish soldier groups from the 1914 war, the edges of the photograph painted in with linked Union Jacks and images of the Crown. They might hang next to a coloured picture of the Queen and the Duke, idealized in *Woman* and torn from this most popular and insipid of magazines. Next to a framed certificate from the Union, too, inscribed with one of those heavy but hopeful mottoes which so largely feature words like 'reason', 'unity' and 'justice'. And then, in the top bedroom, Gladstone, in black-and-white.

Many of the older and apparently most traditionally devout supporters of the Labour Party in places like the Forest of Dean have a double-edged attitude to such things as authority, patriotism, the monarchy and classes other than their own. There is all the expected contempt for the great Godwords used on coins and medals, heard in 1926 and unfurled with flags and government statements. I was in Berry Hill Club the night Princess Margaret's engagement was announced, and though the papers said next morning that there was a great wave of rejoicing 'in the hearts of the ordinary people', the comments of those next to me were unprintable, because one pundit had been tactless enough to explain that she would get an increased allowance when she married. Again there was widespread and uproariously funny derision at one of the Queen's recent Christmas speeches, when she said that 'I know I may seem distant to some of you'. But the disgust at the nobs and some of the more ludicrous aspects of our society is rarely dragged into a total or even understandably comprehensive way of looking at things. Thus, it is not the Queen herself, not the institution of monarchy itself, but the 'hangers on' that draw the fire. The Queen is still confused with the concept of the nation, and the nation is 'us'. The Queen Mother is extremely popular because she is in some recognizable way more 'ordinary', less obviously tainted with the 'them' uniform and mannerisms. 'A real gentleman' is a term of genuine praise, and tends to have a good many of the meanings given to it by some minor but expensive public school. There is no soldier like the British soldier – though, of course, all wars are fought for trade or money no matter what other reasons we might be given. The British have the biggest and best Empire (where Australia and Canada are still 'ours') – but, guiltily, we did keep a lot of others under in the process. Still, it wasn't like the Germans or the Japs.

The ambivalence so characteristic of many of the older working people has become less startling with the younger Foresters. 'Pride' is the one big word that has slid rapidly into a different, looser, context, where it means pride of place, pride of class and pride of nation or even 'race'. These things matter less nowadays: even the Young Conservatives do not talk as though Britain ruled the waves. I've met very few of my generation in the Forest who are taken in by the reasons given for our retention of the Bomb, for instance, for they are much more ready to assume the change in our international status than their parents are. It seems perfectly natural, for instance, that we should get beaten fairly often when we play in international sport. The Bastin or Dean of the older people has become the Didi, de Stefano or Puskas, Fred Perry has become a string of American or Australian names and Henry Cotton now Ben Hogan or Gary Player. My Uncle Fred, in Joyford Hill, once complained bitterly to me about the paucity of our gold medals in the last Olympic Games but one. I said that I thought we had done rather well, on the whole, but he would have none of this.

'We're supposed to be the greatest country in the world, byun us? Well, then, why don't we win as many medals as them Americans?'

Similarly, talk of 'our position', 'our heritage' and so on leaves most of the post-war workers absolutely cold, or embarrassed, or simply amused. There is little of that grudging acceptance of established norms which by degrees had penetrated even into the political language of so many of the older people. At the same time, all the Foresters I know of my age group or younger clearly think that my continued interest in politics is a bit quaint, to say the least. It would be a stupid mistake to call them 'apathetic', in view of their enthusiasms for a whole range of interests and activities that have distinct political consequences, but the whole mechanics of what the papers call 'politics', the posturing of the party leaders and the repetitive wrangles inside the parties, seems part of the structure of yesterday, smells of decay of the past, a response to things that no longer matter so much.

'For the first time,' said Tony Baldwin, who is exactly my age, 'we can breathe a bit. It's possible to do things today without a lot of mumbling in the background, and without being held back all the time. We can become middle-class by our own efforts and our own work, without being holden to anybody.' I knew exactly what he meant, and must admire him for the way he has gone about it — at fifteen he was a labourer in a brick yard, covered in dirt, at twenty-six he is the local under-manager of a building society. Night after night he has slogged away with books and correspondence courses, mastering a new vocabulary, achieving new standards. With it has come change to *The Guardian*, to a new conception of leisure, and to a pleasant flat in Gloucester. What he has done, which is the considerable effort of taking his own life firmly by the scruff of the neck, could hardly have been done even a decade ago. The climate would have worked against it, and a peculiar, clogging and dated 'shame' would have interceded. We both know the source and the power of that shame, and its unfairness. Part of change lies in its use.

At Lydney, on a Saturday night, the young people crowd into the dance, taking a rubber stamp on the hand so that they can go out and return without paying again. Although it was there that I met my wife, I dislike going to dances, always saddened by the boy-trying-to-meet-girl endemic loneliness, competitive loneliness, of such affairs. But now, here, at Lydney Town Hall, surrounded by parked cars, the atmosphere somehow incapsulates the new moods in the Forest of Dean. The faces are relaxed, the bodies are relaxed; there are lots of smiles, and lots of self-confidence. As the girls swirl, slim and carefully dressed, the boys hunt in their packs. A comb is pushed through Brylcreemed hair, cut American style. Trousers taper, shirts are coloured, car keys jangle against the coins.

> *Evening shadows make me blue*
> *When each weary day is through*
> *How I long to be with you*
> *My happiness*

The sax flows downward, and a minute or so later, some coloured balloons float uncertainly downwards into the hot, body-pressing, foot-sliding atmosphere of the dance floor.

'Nora had to have it in her hand, that night.' Sniggers all round. We know Nora. We know.

'That lot over there from Yorkley. The buggers. Stick together, Berry.' Strangely, a form of village pride will break out now and then, and the policeman in the doorway will thumb his jaw, and look less bored.

A scratch dance band from the Forest, faces sweating against the pink light, syncopates a top-twenty number, and another factory earns a royalty. Ploink, *ploink*.

'Did you see Juke-box Jury this evening? Lot of nits.'

The slang is different, the clothes are more metropolitan, and the assumptions or aspirations shifting obliquely through the language would have been unrecognizable to the man who takes tickets at the door. He is not standing close enough, and looks a bit morose.

'Can you get me a Tia Maria?'

'No get thee own.'

'Charmed, I'm sh-oor!'

Later, much later, the cars will start out to climb the hills back on to the central ridge of the Forest.

'Less of your lip,' said a man with a pork-pie hat, scowling at the dancers as they flocked out from the light. He was just looking, just standing, for the pubs had shut and he hadn't gone home. But he resented this other world, and the hard faces. A car door slammed, and an empty cigarette packet plopped on to the pavement. Peter de Stuyvesant. 'So much easier to change to after old-fashioned short cigarettes.'

YOU'LL LOOK A LITTLE LOVELIER EACH DAY
WITH FAB–U–LOUS PINK CAM–AY

And there, in the record shop window, is a big picture of Elvis. G.I. Blues.

'Look at that nigger!'

'Let's drive to Symonds Yat. I've got some beer.'

Off you go, blowing horns through the quiet, darkened villages. Past the abandoned railway station and Park End. Past the sloping rugby ground at Whitecroft. Past the slag heap.

'What a dump!'

HOW DO YOUR NEIGHBOURS RATE YOU?

And tomorrow, my friends, the vicar tells all. He's defrocked now, of course, by the bespectacled Bishop in gaiters.

'That's what I'd do. I'd sell my story.'

'C'mon! C'mon! There's a radio here and all! To the Yat!'

'*What* a dump!'

The headlights switch across the chemist's shop, and we're away.

And yet, in the Forest of Dean, I am still struck by the ways, the scores of deliberate ways, by which people stand aside or despise the commercial standards of this present society, by the multitudes of communal associations and the strengths of the loyalties within them. In a future where 'centralization' will be the key word, heavy with the prospects of international companies, a cartel-bound Europe, billion-pound advertising campaigns, private sky-scrapers, a thousand different brands of cosmetics made by ten companies *et al.*, it is these communal strengths we shall have to protect and expand. They are at the roots of our lives.

What I rather nebulously choose to call 'a sense of community' does seem to involve some degree of conscious opposition to the economic benefits of centralization and mobility, which is its danger, but such a collective yet hardly formulated sense also works against the whole ideology of contemporary capitalism or Welfare State Benthamism, which I see as its virtue. Unfortunately, it is also associated with clogging concepts using the additional sophistication of folksy-wolksy regionalization and mock delegations of authority graced with the name of 'industrial democracy'.

As a result, the habit of thinking in terms of the immediate community, whatever and wherever it may be, has fallen into desuetude. Instead, 'the State' is talked about as if evidence from the different component parts could not affect its universality and its actions. The anonymity of our present nationalized industries, their inability to link up with other social organizations, as in the Forest of Dean with the coal industry, and the large organizations of 'private enterprise' now employing more than 20 per cent of all workers, has led to a changing, centralist structure in our industry. The revolution in transport, in educational needs and large-scale industry has not been compensated for by any fundamental changes in the pattern of our local government or in the relations of those industries, 'public' or 'private', to the regions or towns in which they operate. Again, shop stewards, for example, are attacked because they are in fact operating within a form of primary grouping which is comparatively defenceless on so many counts. Local news-papers are allowed to be owned in chains because they are not thought to be of much importance, because local identity in itself is not thought to be of much importance. Local government is of comparatively minor importance in our political thinking because we've not got round to seeing that its powers and importance depend upon how we value the social unity and strengths of our towns and villages.

We have little or no money to spend on community associations, which have no hope of fulfilling all the functions of which they are capable. Coleford has a very good Community Association, but it cannot give all the help to local activities that it ought to be able to do. They have made sketch plans for a combined Adult and Youth Centre, drawn up with the District Youth Committee, squeezing the maximum possible benefit from the moneys available to both. As in so many other areas, there is plenty of vitality and enthusiasm for such things if they can only be freed from continual poverty of resources, equipment and buildings. I do not think we can over-rate their importance when considering the drift in local life over the past ten years or so, and the 'centralizing' influences that are almost always so commercial and ossifying. Young people are not willing any more to opt for that which is grey and colourless, especially now that they are a special marketing category to be studied, written about and cajoled by those with degrees in psychology working for the advertising agencies.

The so-called Consumers Societies, too, are utterly weak and unimportant, but could be a significant and useful part of the whole as yet unrealized fabric of community life: in fact, the more I see of my own home region in particular, as well as the other places in which I have lived over the last few years, the more I realize that we haven't *begun* to think of how local identity, vitality – call it what you will – can remain a possibility in the face of present developments, of how factory life, housing-estate life, New Town life, can all be aspects of a genuine social, economic and political democracy, based as it must be in the first instance on the primary groupings of the shop floor, the street area, the blocks of new flats and then the village, the town and the big city borough. The people of the Forest of Dean, I can say with more than the usual measure of certainty, obviously and rightly don't want to lose the new things, the easier filling of their lives, but nor do they consciously want to lose the old feelings of 'community', of collective identity and manageable cohesion.

I have described, almost too many times, how nearly every part of the old culture, the old local sense of community, has become suspect, or too weak, diffuse and anachronistic to survive for very much longer. And this, of course, is inevitable: there is nothing unexpected about such developments, and it would be a sign of restriction and economic stagnation if this were not so. But the new commercial kind of substitute for that former way of life does not seem to me to be a *sufficient* change for the better – I feel a kind of indefinable unease, a pity, when I see what has happened and is happening to the Forest of Dean. Describe it how you will, excuse what you will, talk of mobility, opportunity, 'post Capitalism' and 'we are all workers now', I still think that my father's generation has had its dearest hopes and most deserved ambitions betrayed.

EIGHT

The Club is a little way off the crossroads in the lower part of the village, and can easily be located at night by the sound of music and the light thrown in yellow oblongs across the grass from a row of small, eye-level windows. It is a long, low building extended still further at the back by a new, raised hut of fresh timbers, at right angles to the main structure and thus giving the whole place the suitably blasphemous shape of a church. This back hut is an excellent skittle alley, but may also be made available for parties and receptions, where feet thunder on the boards and lots of drink is conveniently near at hand.

Since I know Berry Hill working men's club very well, and since it is an important place in the life of the village, I propose to write about it at length, for here, within one institution and one building, there have been considerable and not always very subtle changes. But I wish I could use two coloured inks to carry on the narrative, switching from one to the other, for I want to indicate changing appearances, to bunch together various impressions taken over seven or eight years of fairly regular attendance. Instead, I want to describe one evening in summer a few years ago, but to bring it up to date as in parenthesis from when I was last there, which, at the time of writing, was just under a month ago.

Inside the main body, the original shell of the club, together with all the normal equipment of an English pub, such as piano, dart board and domino sets, there are membership charts, pictures of the last Gloucestershire County rugby fifteens to have had Berry Hill men in the team, and a large, drawing-pin perforated notice board for the perennial club events – the children's outing (1961: Barry), the old age pensioners' fund, the committee elections and announcements, and the proposals (with names of seconder) for new memberships. There is also a large polished radiogram and, on a corner shelf, a smoky-grey face of a television set (BBC only). Its most regular time of operation is for 'Sportsview' on Wednesday nights during the football seasons.

Now, 1961, the set is twenty-one inch, and takes commercial television as well. The rugby pictures have been taken down, presumably because no one is interested enough in them. The walls have been redecorated in a couple of pastel shades of blue and with a high-gloss paint. And near the bar is the latest innovation: a one-armed bandit. Put in sixpence, the machine whirls and clicks, and you might get the jack-pot. 'Sixpence taken there,' the secretary told me, 'is worth more to the club than sixpence taken over the bar.' 'A fool and his money is soon parted,' added Mr Gallaher, 'the makers didn' put it there to give money away.'

It was a Saturday in a warm enough June. The sun was sliding through the little curtained windows in wide, dusty shafts, splashing on to the nearest tables to improve the colours and prints on the beer mats. I was very dry, having walked up from Coleford, a couple of miles over the hill, and since lagers or cold beers were then unobtainable, I was drinking warm bitter and sweating uncomfortably in the process. (You can get lager now.) There were few members in the club, because of the heat and because it was still early in the evening: half a dozen old men, Mr Dorrington behind the bar, Harvey Harris the secretary, and myself. Margaret and my parents were coming up at a more respectable hour.

The old men sat around the big, army-type stove, a winter habit that had gradually stretched throughout the year: the stove is not lit, of course, and they are not gathered round it just to wait or merely to remember. Their progress through the day is punctuated with more precise habits, that is all – the time they get up, where they walk, where they sit and what they eat. They are immune to, or cannot afford, the newer restlessness and anxiety about possessions and habits: as far as the old people are concerned, the old culture persists, for are they not still alive? Veined, heavily lined hands lay across the tables, circle into the handles of the pints. They drank 'level' with each other, nicely sociable. Their voices appeared to me to ramble off on a series of tangents, dealing in experiences younger or even middle-aged people could not possibly have shared. If one were attempting to paint the old men in the club, and not merely take a photograph, as people set vividly in a particular environment, one would, suddenly, be confused by *which* environment, for the past not only bends their backs and callouses their hands, but moves heavily in their minds, their limbs and their whole language and outlook. They seem to have gone too near the cold centre: poverty, superstition, fatalism, narrowness, intolerance were there, and yet, at the same time, they are linked to each other by more than the passage of time, for there is amongst them a compelling warmth, a certainty and a strength which is clear in almost everything they say. Nowadays, they would be called 'cussed', and it would take more than a 'labour relations' course to subdue them.

Despite the sun, some of them are wearing short, knitted pull-overs, and, of course, the usual flat, peaked caps. And the usual smoke shrouds their talk. I moved across and sat with them, a bit nervously. What does *thik* want? Is he going to ask *questions*? I tried not to.

I sat next to the Lodge brothers, 'Farmer' and Alan, both in their sixties, well-built, powerful and good-humoured men. Both had the cap and pull-over, and 'Farmer' had his customary twig in the corner of his mouth. Alan Lodge used to play rugby for Gloucestershire and the British Army – as a forward, of course. He speaks very slowly, and one is never quite sure whether he is joking or not, savouring each word with the rather laboured but delightful care of a pedant. Occasionally, he will talk about rugby, always sure of an attentive audience for this at least. To strangers, he is invariably pointed out as 'that's Alan. Used to play rugby for Gloucestershire and the British Army. Listen to the woy a' do talk,' so much so that I find I have done the same thing.

Perhaps to put me at my ease (I was then playing fairly regularly in the local rugby colours, black and amber) he was telling me of some rough-and-tumble incident from his long-distant playing career. He thought the present lot of players were a bit soft on the edges, without the fire and the local pride, the total enthusiasms he had known. Forest of

Dean rugby teams were renowned and feared for the vigour and speed of their forward play, and the pack was all – not for them the unpredictable flashes of individualism more suited to the temperament of the Welsh a few miles away. The local cry, I was told, used to be 'breathe on 'um, Berry'. Alan had reached the point in his reminiscence where the trainer had rushed on to the field to double-up a semi-conscious player of the other side, believing him to be winded. 'Sponge his neck, mon,' a contrite Alan had whispered, 'that's where I hit 'n.' As way of explanation, and perhaps apology, it was explained that 'when we went down there (into Wales), it was to – ah – (and his lips smacked) – a HOSTILE SETTLEMENT'.

Delighted, I provoked further rugby talk. The game itself seemed a natural expression of the old Forest way of life, being tough, masculine, village-centred, collective and yet self-expressive, a thing from which the women were excluded. To wear the black and amber jersey of Berry Hill used to be the summit of a local man's pride and lordship, a gift to swagger with and live on every day of the week, not just Saturdays. At this time, the rugby team was already in difficulties (else I wouldn't have got into the side) and attendances were down considerably, if still respectable. Attendances have gone down even further since. And the teams at Littledean, Ruspidge, Lydbrook, Ruardean have disappeared, Drybrook and Whitecroft packed up for a time, and the remainder exist on perhaps one tenth of their former support. It is even difficult to get fifteen players together for an away game. Part of the decline lies in the crumbling of village pride and autonomy, but mostly it is due to the growing habit of turning elsewhere, of avoiding the older, communal pursuits, and the coming of television, with

'Grandstand' on BBC on Saturday afternoons. Once, the keenest of the miners so placed by the shift system would rush straight from a Saturday morning work stint to the rugby ground, to put vaseline on their ears and pull on the broad-striped, challengingly colourful garb of the many local rugby teams the district produced.

Jim Hale, his back bent from a severe pit accident, downed his pop and cider, and with sudden, energetic relish, a louder voice and livelier eyes, told about some of his great battles down in the valley of the hostile settlements. 'The last time I played for Berry Hill down in Wales,' he said, 'thoy finished up wi' fower of their players on the touchline. Nor thoy couldn't walk whum as easily as we could!' In the same game, it appears, a 'sly little Welshman' had been put out of action for a longer period than just that particular match – a longer period, in other words, than was ethical. Half-heartedly I remonstrated that surely that would have been going a bit too far? but sank back, grinning and defeated, when he brought out a phrase which justified everything: 'Well, mind, him had the ball!'

The talk began to fall away, to become sentimental, as it nearly always does when people start recalling a shared past, and attention was driven from words and facial expressions to eyes partially filmed over by the efforts of remembering and the burdens of nostalgia.

But in the club that evening, listening, talking, just being there, I felt a bit moved, and very much at home. Perhaps it was just the sun, the long, hot summer days. Outside, the grass seemed made of a thicker, more shadowy pile, growing down into the earth instead of sprawling along its bumpy surface like paint, as earlier in the day when the sun had been overhead. We talked more of rugby, then the band and then the chapel. I felt myself being ducked head-first into the past, hearing its sounds and turning within it, carefully prompted by the old men around me. I learnt that the Whitsun recitations by the children at Salem had been well attended, the chapel full of parents in best clothes listening proudly or nervously to their children, new shoes creaking, new clothes starchy and flowered, swaying a little as they said their pieces while the same clock ticked on, heavily. Some village intelligence, the continual flow of public discussion, sooner or later tells you all you need to know.

Now there is a gang of cars parked outside the club. It is cooler, the place is filling up. Outside, too, it is a bit duskier, thickening here and there into clouds of gnats to promise another fine, hot day.

I was lucky. Along the ashen path between the council houses the band had made its approach. 'On the Quarter Deck', rousing enough, and a late concert on the tufty grass at the club's entrance. This doesn't happen very often nowadays. The men came out with their pints of warm beer, and that old respect on their faces. The band, the band, the band rustle the voices, delighted. Children play with tennis balls, and circle the band in screaming pleasure, children who are better dressed, bigger, and so much healthier than those of two decades before. The tourist, again, would enjoy this, and be tempted to take photographs. I wanted to remember this, too, feeling a little overwhelmed at being able to stand before a chunk of 'the past'. Hearing the music, and standing outside the club with Margaret and my parents, it seemed too much the summer, too idyllic, too much the Forest of Dean I have known and loved. For I knew, as well, that the pits are closing, the club is losing members, the chapel is falling away, the rugby team cannot always get a full fifteen, and the Foresters are closing up in front of each other as never before. And that many young people want to leave, as I have left. 'There's nothing to kip 'um here, o'butty.' The times I have heard that said, started to disagree, then checked myself for a hypocrite. There is too much truth in it, but for all who have grown up here and speak the language of the place, there is also too much that is callous and hopeless in it.

The band has formed into a circle, still playing, the finishing sun flashing at angles upon the high polish of silver instruments, and the buttons and buckles of the bandsmen's uniforms. Mr Hartley is conducting, a wisp of greyish hair working loose, his spectacles also caught like windows in the sun. They finish the march with a brassy flourish, and the listeners clap and nod at each other.

'Very nice. Let's have another.'

A few people are out in the back gardens of the near-by council houses, still in shirt-sleeves.

'Washing thik car? Agyun?'

'Play some more.'

Half a mile away, the woods are cooled by shadow, occasionally penetrated by shafts from the gleam beyond. The beer tastes frothily warm, and it is all very, very pleasant.

The band had stopped playing by the time the light-grey summer dusk had swept in from the distance, blotting out the Welsh mountains and the bluer Malvern hills and removing the polished depths, the circled images, shining on the cars outside the iron gate. It had become chilly, the incredulous shiver after a warm day, and, as always, the wind was beginning to rise, drawn through and buffeted by the hills and slopes and thousands of tall trees. The light from the Club was now brighter and splashed across a greater distance.

A minor but irritating tribulation of my life is that after three or four pints of beer I start to hiccup, quite loudly, for a short period only, and then, as if it were a second wind, they go, and I am free to give myself a headache for the next morning. So, when I talked to some of the men in the band, putting their stiff, grubby music cards away for the next practice night, I began, blast it, to hiccup.

'Hold thee nose, o'but,' someone said, winking at those nearest him, making me feel nicely ridiculous. Margaret abandoned me with a laugh and went into the rapidly filling and much noisier Club with my mother and father. I began, dreadfully, to feel like a sociologist, a questioner with a hiccup.

'I'll be alright after another couple.'

'Doosn't worry, ol' un,' a pale face laughed, braided cap tilted backwards, 'thee dad used to have far wuss than hiccups with the beer he sunk when he used to come along wi' us.'

The band used to be in constant demand, and the men who belonged to it had, again, thought themselves possessors of a massive and enviable privilege: on a par with the black-and-amber. Then, there were regular concerts, local contests, marching for the chapel behind the tasselled admonitory banner, the rugby ground occasions, and coach trips to play in a pub back-room or walled garden. A few years ago, the band was all but finished and nearly closed down, hanging together by habit and the paid-up existence of uniforms, music cards and instruments. It was rescued by the enthusiasm and energy of a new conductor, Harold Hartley. Talking, as it were, against the clock, coaxing, making jokes, training newcomers, he has virtually re-created the band. Always there are individuals strong enough or earnest enough to go against the stream. But beyond the practice room, which, even when empty seems capable of making a metallic, bell-like sound and smells of leather straps and brass, the newly revived band could not hope to achieve again its former status in the village. An elegy would be a likelier sound.

Every Christmas, still, the band moves from each cluster of houses in the district, playing carols and getting drinks and coppers from the doors and gates of the listening families. This is a valuable source of revenue, for since the decline or removal of the public activities with which the band was associated, they are, like the rugby club and the chapel, short of money. I wonder, too, how many Christmas times are left, the blowing in the cold, gripping whitefingered on the freezing brass and stamping cold feet in between the change of music cards.

'I'd like to see the band at Christmas, mind. We'd turn the wireless down a bit and give um something to drink.'

Inevitably, the band feels itself more of a separate unit, less a vital part of a larger, more integrated whole: there are no village carnivals and chapel galas at which to play, and it does not turn out at the rugby ground for a Forest derby. Most of the energy goes now in qualifying and being placed at contests beyond the Forest, like some of those minor amateur London soccer clubs which play only away games.

Back in the Club, crowded now, shut away from the rising breeze, I asked my father if he had enjoyed his years in the band, an unnecessary question perhaps, but strangely one I had not asked him before. With a characteristic gesture, he drew his pint along the table top in a wet circle before answering, a sure sign of embarrassment.

'Oy, I did. We had some good times, and it was sort of important, then. I've blown till my lips were too cracked to drink properly.' He caught a glance from my mother and, ruefully, added, 'not that that stopped me, mind.' Once, he said, they played from nine o'clock one Boxing morning until way past tea time without going home for dinner and the collection boxes were almost too heavy to hold.

Why, then, did he leave? Why did Jack Hawkins leave? Why did Tony Baldwin, his brother Bob, and Haydn Harris leave? A vague, worried frown, an inability to say, exactly, why. 'I dunno really. It don't seem the same somehow. Chunt like it used to be,' and, finally, in exasperation at my obtuseness, 'well, *thou's* know!'

The answers are almost always like this, appeals to a shared knowledge or silence about the difference between 'then' and 'now' except for comparisons of prosperity and talk of the past as something unrelated to the present, offering no comments for it. In the Forest of Dean it is as if you could feel the life changing under your feet like a mild but sustained tremor, changing habits and lives as if climatically, introducing a fresh 'permanence'. There is, as a result, besides the vigour of the new and the sturdy feeling of prosperity and new opportunity, an air of decay, an apologetic sense of loss and an almost truculent (but rarely spoken) willingness to acknowledge it, as if it reflected personally upon each one that had made his life in the district. *Other* people should still go to chapel, should care about the band, should go and watch the rugby, there are *reasons* why *I* can't go, and so on. The new generation does not even stand at one remove, with slight guilt or hesitancy and nagging memory: they act, in dress, style, mannerisms, with a studied, casual earnestness, as if cast in the role of the innocent and necessary plunderer. In the New Towns, in Bethnal Green, in Cheltenham and Barrow-in-Furness they belong to the same cause and are forced to worship the same images, but, perhaps because I am one of them, I feel hopeful and strangely certain about them, left as they are without hard, driving dogmas and with a youth which kicks against acceptance and apathy, against old words and dead emotions. The angel makers, the 'pop' managers, the teen-page writers, the ad-men and the chain-store board rooms have done their best to make 'youth' (the 'young idea', the teen beano) a commercial word, while local magistrates, ageing Union officials and the 'respectable' from the privet hedges have made it a defensive concept. So here, too, in the Forest of Dean there has been a sizeable increase in the 'juvenile delinquency' rate and tut-tutting of machine-gun-like proportions. We cannot respond to something that is, if not dead, certainly at a strung-out pitch of exhaustion.

But now, tonight, 'exhaustion' would be just about the most inappropriate word one could possibly find. On the surface, there is still enough light to dazzle the eyes. The Club is full, the coolness, the dusk and the habit have drawn people from their square stone houses and newer council models to this chattering, hustling, beer-smelling centre, a palace that is narrow and wide, a hub of intolerance and generosity, full of vitality and decency, yet also of monotony and an accumulated, ritualized deadness.

To get from the door to the bar, the altar end of the church, a member has to walk right through the long, low building by an open passage between the sets of tables and the people who have already arrived. It is impossible to do this inconspicuously: the idea of a 'private bar', of segregated drinking, is an alien one in this place. All the older communal activities have this feeling of openness and unadorned collectivity, where 'individual' status signs are not recognized, nor needed. The unconventional, the unorthodox, the strange and the withdrawn were likely to be butts in the past, but never in quite the same hostile fashion as those who sought to contract out for social reasons or attempted to bargain with their employers on an individual basis. A man who sought to haul coal with a horse and cart during the 1926 strike was killed on one of the sharp Forest slopes when his cart overturned, and it was almost as if the martial, labour-minded God of the chapels had shown his hand.

As the door of the Club opens, especially if it is still fairly early in the evening, the heads of those already inside snap up like poppies in the rain to take a look at who is coming through. If an unfamiliar face hesitates at the door there is a slight hum of questioning. 'Who's that, then?' Everyone must be placed and measured, talked about and, frequently and gratuitously, judged. It can therefore be a minor but an irritating ordeal to walk up this cluttered aisle, particularly if you have offended some group loyalty or susceptibility, or if you are 'carrying on' with someone else's wife or are known to keep your children in an unkempt or ill-mannered condition. 'Where do him work now?' 'Who the hell do her think her is?' and 'Ant sin him in here for some time, ast thou? – Course, a' got a car now, an' a? And they d'cost more than bottle tops to kip!'

People also sit, if they can, in regular seats, in established positions. Old Mr Hale sits next to the piano on the side nearest the door, the Lodge brothers round the stove, and my family almost always between the radiogram and the bar, for example. A deliberate succession of recognizable similarities is built up as part of the ritual, carefully reaching out for the ideal of talk and habit and amusement which can best fill a local man's life, echoing vague collective desires, and satisfying, for an evening, personal conceptions of contentment and community, the purple before the drab inevitability of Monday and work again. It is known who is likely to be in the Club and where they will probably be sitting on any evening of the week, and there might almost be an agenda of subjects for discussion. But, physically, the contours are changing, and the activities inside will gradually be altered as a result. The walls have been newly decorated with an eggshell blue colouring which looks earnestly contemporary, new curtains have been put up and someone has taken down the notice in the gents which said, very much to the point, 'Please Pee in the Trough.' For a period you could buy expensive, saloon-bar style Keg Bitter and there is a wider range of soft drinks. Plans have been made to yank out the fat old stove and put in less obtrusive radiators instead. And yet new clothes are not quite enough, for the air of ritualized predictability remains, surviving the change of physical surroundings rather as a snail would survive the dusting and colouring of its shell.

The young people in Berry Hill, therefore, will not admit to finding the Club either as attractive or as necessary as their

III

parents do. The television, the three-speed radiogram, the new curtains and the egg-shell fragility of the wall colouring is seen just as a ridiculous camouflage, ultimately changing nothing of substance and altering few intentions. On Saturday and Sunday nights, it is true, there are many young families sitting at the tables, where tomato juice or bitter lemon is drunk as well as beer or cider, and pop records turn on the radiogram. But they are a minority, and a diminishing one, out of trend with the larger impetus of the under-thirties (a convenient enough watershed), where the word 'community' is more like the advertising word 'together-ness'. The older concept is dismissed as drab and dull, out of touch, and, devastatingly, 'not with it'. Of course, the Club is not alone in this: the band, the chapel and even the rugby team suffer the same venomous condemnations, so, in a less distinct and immediate fashion, do the trade unions and the local Labour Party, which have seemed to be the political extensions, the intellectualization, of this older culture now being rejected so utterly. The *attempt* at rejection, anyway, can be described as determined and unqualified, but we still speak with its accent and cannot completely free ourselves from the former way of living. This is no big city, where the neon can easily and flashily confirm the changes, harden the decisions, and the sense of intimacy and conservatism is muted and dispersed by the acres of streets and the loosening of contact beyond the places of work, but a district of hills and trees, ever-present beauty, small villages and village-like towns where, although 'modernity' can be seen a mile off, everywhere and tenaciously, the previous structures and habits surround it, change it and, for the moment, in the eyes of the young, appears always to conquer. Retreating and conquering, withdrawing and yet stubbornly ubiquitous, the old Forest of Dean is still there to be observed. Because it is still alive, albeit with a gasp, the young still see only the consequent frustration, the bones and not the flesh of it, and we are unable to sort it out and see what made it so powerful and so narrow. The changes have been too sudden, too much in contradiction to what was valuable in the traditions and habits of a working class so long on the defensive that we stumble a little under the onslaught of the new exploiters.

'Well, what can you do?' asked Harvey Harris, the secretary of the Club and son of the Salem preacher, spreading an arm to take in the tables and the newly decorated Club. 'The young people just don't want it, and that's all there is to it. We're finished as far as they are concerned.' There was a finality in his voice which could only have come after long and unhappy thought, for he works extremely hard in his spare time to keep the Club alive in every sense that is left to it. He has, wearily, tried to give up the job on several occasions, but the elected committee will not hear of it, for they know that nowadays there is a shortage of people prepared to work for such things – the rugby club has had the same difficulties finding committee-men prepared to turn up at meetings (or even matches!), keep the team running and filling the fixture lists; the chapel cannot get good visiting speakers and the Labour Party cannot get new members or enthuse the older ones with its purpose. Few are prepared to tinker for long with a machine that is too obviously running down. There are by now too many doubts about the old culture and the former values of the Forest of Dean, doubts that can, of course, be valuable and emancipating, but also exist as a deadening, stupefying process, the thing which is making England such a confused and unhappy mixture of dynamism and lethargy, with priorities so questionable and politics so quiescent.

I was recently shown the membership books for the past few years of the Club's existence, my eyes aided by Harvey's finger as it stabbed angrily across the wide pages of the ledgers. In the period he was talking about there had been the most pronounced of the increases in local prosperity, a time of 'no deposit' hire purchase and the beginnings of commercial television. The juke-boxes had come to Coleford, two miles over the hill, and school-leavers were beginning to earn the kind of money which would have seemed impossible less than a decade before. And as Harvey's finger moved down the neatly penned columns, all these things loomed behind the completed pages as if to explain and mock, putting the Club and all associated with it in their proper places.

Two hundred people have withdrawn their membership in the last half dozen years, and many more have stopped coming, except for a drink at Christmas or to a particularly good concert. Worse, as far as the Club is concerned, younger people are not even bothering to join and have a look at the place.

One of the reasons why this happens is (for this area) a new and rapidly developing feeling for the symbols and gradings of a sense of status amongst many of the younger men and women of the Forest and a good many of the pre-war generations as well. This, of course, is not a surprising thing, for the search for 'status' as a value itself, the need to possess and flaunt the right things and the necessity for doing what is currently 'correct' at the proper times and in the proper place has perhaps become the dominant concern of contemporary advertising, gossip columnists and marketing experts.

I have talked to many of my age in Berry Hill and its immediate district who spoke of the Club not just as if it were, in their opinion, drab and old-fashioned, but also as if it were socially lowering, something to be a bit ashamed of, a place to laugh at – not necessarily in a braying, arrogant fashion, but with a tinge of pity and contempt. It will be pointed out that the potato crisps are given to you in a bag, and not emptied on to a plate; you would not be given a knife with a wrapped pork pie; and walking up the long aisle between the peering, nosy tables is 'like walking the plank'. I'm certainly inclined to agree with this latter description, never having myself managed the action without some discomfort and self-consciousness. Also, some of my contemporaries will insist with truth that the Club is one long room, in effect, where everyone congregates without any 'privacy' and where you can never be sure whether you are sitting where someone else had already acquired a claim through longer usage, whereas in 'The White Hart' at Coleford, for example, or 'The Feathers' at Lydney, there are certainly dart-boarded and planky public bars, but there are also comfortable, hotel-like lounges with chairs of living-room respectability and, in one, a collection of deep-flickering, warm brass resting on polished wood. There are bowls of flowers, carpets and best bitter in half-pints or glasses, as well as discreet, properly printed notices advertising, say, a barbecue given by the local Young Conservatives or a dinner dance at Lydney, Chepstow or Gloucester.

Most of these comments and objections are perfectly obvious and straight-forward, of course, and there seems little virtue in making drabness synonymous with dignity and a certain kind of political ethic. But the way they are formulated, the way I have always heard them, adds a further, less obvious or pleasant dimension. There is the patronizing lift of the head, the forced laughter about 'the old Foresters', relegating them to yokel-like comedians in the manner of British films, and an obsessive, sick desire to tabulate places, people and things (or even ideas and political attitudes) according to some carefully determined hierarchical pattern. The result is a loss of sympathy, a set of closed standards of behaviour. For Christ's sake use words like 'lunch' and 'table napkin', and, above all, be careful, be on your guard, for there are so many traps. Some fish, it appears, are served with their tails in their mouths. The *Daily Telegraph* and the *Sunday Times* are becoming more popular with my contemporaries because 'culture' itself is a great tabulator, and, demonstrably, is connected with the 'right ways' in a very immediate, if occasionally esoteric fashion.

I remember talking to a friend about a dinner for the Berry Hill rugby club, and the logical place to have it, with drinks, was in Berry Hill itself. This would have meant holding it in either the Club or 'The Globe', a hundred yards away and the nearest pub to the rugby ground itself.

'We don't want to have a spread at "The Globe",' Dave said, emphatically, and with a slight tone of incredulity at the very suggestion.

'Well why not? That's where we always go before the match, isn't it?'

'But that's different. You'd want something better than that if you can. All them old blokes around, those days are finished. We'd want it more like a proper social club nowadays. You couldn't bring a girl, a nice girl, to a place like "The Globe" or the Club, now could you?'

I don't want to be unfair, and there is a lot to be said for such attitudes, since the desire for self-improvement and a wish to acquaint oneself with wider, freer and 'better' things have long been the only likely incentives for certain people in the working classes who think of emancipation in the eternity of one-by-one achievement. Undoubtedly, the Forest is a more open society and a more liberal one than it used to be, it remains a nice place in which to live: but it grates when I hear the rhythms of a cash-register and status-hypnotized way of speech here, of all places, because there are enough reasons and sufficient signs left to make one aware of the other alternatives, to realize that this need not have been so, that the 'social revolution' might have grown in other, less imprisoning ways.

NINE

Saturday night. There's nothing quite like it for heating the blood. It is the great day, the release day, and a long way off Monday morning. In working-class England, things liven up on a Saturday – and yet, I suppose, to a stranger the ugly, fly-blown, splotchy mirrored pubs can seem the most boring and unwholesome places in town.

I'll go back a little, once more, to that same evening. Since it is eight o'clock, the Club is now almost full, clouding rapidly with the drifts of tobacco smoke, noisy with chatter, coughing and laughing, all of which seem half a pitch above the normal. At that time my mother was playing the piano at week-ends, but she doesn't sing as a solo performer any more, which is perhaps just as well for when she used to my father would shout 'order, order', and glare round with quite venomous hostility at those who dared to make the slightest or most unavoidable sounds during 'Bless This House' or 'The Lost Chord'. Quite right, too.

It is still too early for community singing in anything but the most spasmodic and half-hearted of fashions, and the piano merely plonks through the talk and the guzzling as the necessary prelude, the reminder of things to come and voices yet to be heard. Meanwhile, I can gaze round the Club like the rest, and try to describe some of its impact, an impact which survives the predictability and even the passages of monotony. I astonished myself by realizing that I knew by name all but seven or eight people in the hall, and knew most of them as adults when I was a child. They confirm the past, for me and for themselves, unwilling to change too much lest they loosen their hold on events and hopes they do not want to forget. Or maybe it is simply a matter of habit.

There are two families opposite who probably have no great affection for each other, but who have a dual identity in the eyes of the others in the Club. They are often caught making unkind or deliberately malicious comments about each other, where none were called for, but, as far as the other villagers are concerned, they remain as thick as thieves, 'round each other's houses at all hours of the day', phrases which the families in question also use, sniffily, about a score or more similar relationships. Familiarity also breeds gossip and such situations as these, and I do not want to slide over with conveniently romantic words the intolerance and local chauvinism which were also characteristic of the Forest of Dean. The talk in the Club would not allow a visitor to escape that impression whatever else he might miss: 'You can see, too, the way so-and-so over there is looking at so-and-so's wife, can't you – there! see! he lit her cigarette.'

'Yunt that the dress her sister used to wear – well, if it chunt, I'll bet that's somebody else's hand-downs any road.'

'Look, that's five pints already, and it chunt barely eight o'clock itt.'

'Oy, thou bist right, ol' un, him do want a good butt ash round the arse on in, and him ool get it one day, see if I byunt right!'

'A lovely fellah, oy, him is that, wouldn't hurt a flea. Not unless the bugger were bighting him.'

'That's the trouble with this country, too many blacks and foreigners.'

'Why should my money help pay family allowance and subsidise somebody else's bed – we never had it in our day.'

'Where bist working now then, Harold? Off from here a bit en it?'

'Oy, the other side of Cardiff. On the Gloucester road.' One gets the impression that even London is on the Gloucester road. All roads are built from here, are measured from here.

Gradually, the individual talk spreads across the tables and becomes a little mellower; the small, mainly family groupings break up a little; the unkindnesses appear to be swallowed up with the beer, a process as speedy as their birth; people lean across in new and temporary alliances, and the babble rises into a smoky whole, rubbing against the walls and ignoring even those who have just come in and are soberly walking the plank. If I were a known adulterer, this would be the time I would come and get my drink.

The bell rings and Brian Harris, the dark, slim, lean-faced captain of the rugby team, makes an announcement about the forthcoming children's outing to Porthcawl. This seems to confirm that the Club is by this time no longer a collection of units and small groups, nor even a convenient centre for gossip, but alive again. Announcements are never made too early, no matter how many might be there. There are a lot of the older people here, cloth capped and with teeth missing, being exactly as they always have been, utterly oblivious to the objections their sons and daughters might have to this place and to all that they consider part of themselves. They could not care a miner's cuss about the existence elsewhere of Elizabethan eating houses and cocktail sausages with little sticks in their middles, and I once blamed them for it with a genuine dislike. It is difficult for young men on the make to come to terms with those who have made their experiences, largely harsh and crushing ones at that, into apparently manageable coatings of their own personalities. They cannot be taken in so easily as a lifetime of being bullied and deceived would indicate, if I may use a paradox which seems to be true. Their strength (or, if you must, their prejudices) would be unaffected by the so-called electoral swing and the political enthusiasm for the *status quo* alleged to have been released by the birth of the Queen's third child or the long hot summer prior to the election Mr Macmillan won. They have been through wars and strikes, poverty and what seemed comparative affluence with the final, inescapable conviction that the great division between 'them' and 'us' still persists, that their real interests (i.e. the interests they consider important) are still of little significance, and that the things they respond to, and regard as life-giving, William Hickey & Co would think of far less concern than news of the deb who dyed her hair wet-copper-green, or whatever it was. That old woman, fussing unknowingly with her swollen knuckled hands and plucking at her voluminous skirt, does not expect to be as well treated as a pedigree race horse or a Mayfair poodle.

The solo singing has at last begun and there is an attentive, expectant shuffle, with a lot of 'sh'-ing across the laden tables, still clinking with glasses and bottles. Some of the songs are the latest that can be bought in the record shops or heard on Juke-box Jury, others are the older, more sentimental and beery kind, sung with a gusto sufficient to remove any spurious nostalgia which might have softened the eyes of those bellowing their memories. Both kinds are assimilated into a common type, so that 'She Was Only a Bird In a Gilded Cage' or 'She Was Only Six-teen, On-ly Six-teen' sound as though they might have been written by the same person. As with so many other things, both physical and emotional, the task of occupying and transforming, of making safe, has to be undertaken, making it possible and predictable, removing the more blatantly alien fragments and injecting the familiar at all levels and in all circumstances. I have noticed the same process at work in some of the large, smelly pubs of Fulham and Hammersmith in London, emphasized there by the huge mirrors and ornate fittings reflecting back a lingering oppressiveness of Victorian proportions. There is, in working-class England, maybe held below the surface, a residual but still massive *fear* of change, no matter what kind, for better or worse, since change cannot be as certain and the more disastrous kind has often been heralded as 'better'. As one of the results, working-class culture is obviously cautious, fairly conservative and, it will appear at times, too much on the look-out, suspicious of the forces which tend to pull it apart, splintering the precious, the necessary unity in a thousand different dangers. This characteristic, above everything else, throws up the barriers between the generations and leaves the young, reasonably prosperous worker so much adrift, so anarchic, and so vulnerable to the persuasions many of the older ones continue to resist with such vigour and gloriously unashamed hostility. In one-class areas, like the Forest of Dean or South Wales, I sometimes, and exaggeratedly, get the feeling that so clouded with differing traditions and assumptions has outside contact between the generations become that a real dialogue between the two has become impossible: it is almost as if the alphabet and the script has changed. Sometimes, anyway.

The singers are called up to the small platform jutting out in front of the piano by the Club's chairman, Mr Bill Gallaher, a miner who moved many years ago from South Wales to the Forest of Dean, like many others in both directions. He is not very tall, but heavily built, and has a jaunty, fluty voice suiting the angle of his cap and the bright, pleasant look on his face. The voice easily clears a way through the still thickening banks of smoke and perpetual, between-songs bustle.

'Ladies and gentlemen! Ladies and gentlemen, *if* you please, *if* you please! The next artist, by popular request is . . .', and the names go on, people who have been given the sole right to sing certain favourite numbers which must not then be sung by anyone else. There is a pleasurable air of promise, varying according to who gets on the platform and the barometer of his popularity, irrespective of the quality of his voice. My father will admit that he has a terrible voice, but he always manages to get some of the heartiest and warmest applause. Such a response flows between the performer and his audience in an alive, exhilarating manner, a way which might soon be lost in echo chambers and parallel recording microphones.

> There's an old, old app-ul tree out in the orchard
> That will live for ev-er in my-y-y mem-or-ee
> It reminds me of my pappy, who was Handsome,
>   young and happ-ee
> When he planted this old, old app-ul tree.

That's Harold Grindle's song, and he sings it with the strained suspiciously innocent face of a worried cherub or a depraved angel; no one else would dare sing it, because no one else could possibly sing it so well or so tenderly. But all join in, raucous and arm-beating 'old apple tree! old apple tree! It reminds me of my pappy, who was handsome, young and happy, When he planted THE OLD APP-UL TREE.' Slap, slap.

Sooner or later there comes a breather, a welcome pause, time to cluster urgently at the top end, round the bar, to discover who else has come in now that the Club is too full to seat everybody without an amount of shuffling and squeezing up into corners. Mum continues to thump away on the piano, because people are by now willing to take up and sing the tunes she is playing. Eventually, there will have to be 'Bread of Heaven' as in Wales (but do not say so) – a beerily religious incantation, evangelical and powerful. The few children in the place are reminded of chapel, but by now are heavy-eyed, half asleep over bottles of pop, too tired to race round the tables and get in the way, too tired even to ask questions. And those who are regularly more high-spirited, or more vulnerable to drink, 'the groite fools' are swaying visibly under cap or soft trilby. There might, too, be the more jagged sounds of argument, flaring swiftly and blazing throughout the week. But the days of the running fist-fights and inter-village brawls have almost disappeared; life is gentler, less 'masculine' and, for the less orthodox, the less group-conscious, more tolerable.

The interval is over, and Mr Gallaher again rings the bell over the piano, setting his face into that of the important and patient impresario. Cyril Baglin is called, and already the audience is beginning to laugh in anticipation, as a studio audience when it sights the boiled-greens, podgy face of Tony Hancock. Cyril is undoubtedly one of the most gifted and fanciful comedians I have ever listened to. But Baglin's humour could not be transplanted, for it is intensely and devastatingly local in accent, pace and subject matter. Each region of England still has its songs and comedians, its superstitions and prides, but we shall soon be collecting these on gramophone records before the flatness rolls over. In the Forest of Dean, the rhythms of life and speech still demand the concentration uniqueness demands, and if this book appears to be too close to its subject, too concerned with the minutiae of a district's life, this is because I feel it is extremely difficult to translate the core of a retreating, narrowing community life when so many of our current social and political assumptions make no provision for anything but folksey, lore-like sympathy with the victims or the benefi-ciaries of such changes. Eurovision seems much more marvellous.

Cyril is on his feet. The last time I brought a friend to the Club, on his first visit to the Forest of Dean, he was completely lost with the speed and close, regional splatterings of the patter, but the obvious, almost ecstatic joy of everyone around him was almost enough compensation. My sister's boy friend works in Bristol and was born in London, and when he comes down every other week-end or so, and Cyril happens to be performing at the Club, he is constantly leaning across to June, demanding 'What was that? What did he say? What was that last bit? What the hell are they laughing at now?' But she can never explain.

Baglin is short and natty, with a boyish face and soft, short fair hair. He stretches on the balls of his feet when making a point, and like many good, fast-talking comedians, uses his hands as dilated muscles of his tongue. He also is gifted with a fine sense of timing, so that the delivery of something which would read, at best, as only mildly amusing, or even obscene, is brilliant enough to make it seem hilarious and true. If anyone has the misfortune or mis-directed sense of confidence to walk in while Baglin is performing, he is made the butt of a series of remarks swiftly feeding on the laughter created by the preceding ones.

'Well tha see,' Cyril was explaining, with a slight air of condescension, as if he were admitting that it was necessary to give a little background for those who did not want to be plunged straight into the body of a joke, 'it was up the top of Berry Hill – the last place God made – and then him had to apologize – anyway, it was in the lanes, when we had thik horrible thick fog last wik.' He pauses momentarily, and a few people started to nod their agreement. Yes, that's right, there was a fog last week. . . .

'And these mon – well, him were selling educational books – Encyclist's and Old Moore's, and, of course, 'im hadn't been to Berry Hill afore. Hinterland, see. And he was looking for old Thomas' house, in the lanes.'

Yes, they knew the one. It was dark there at night thanks to the tall hedges. How nice to have a joke about nice old Thomas.

'Some silly bugger had told'n Thomas could read. But him still couldn't see a thing. *Not* a thing. Except 'a could make out a shaft of light behind what must a bin a door of some sart. So him went up to these door and knocked.'

Cyril was telling it with a lowered voice now, arms still for once, and there was undoubtedly a gradual inexplicable feeling of drama being built up despite the fact that he had said so little.

'Him waited a bit. Nothing happened at first, so a knocked agyun. Then there was a slight rustle. And the door creaked open just a bit – just a crack, madam, just a crack – and he could make out as twere a little boy poking his yud round the door. Thomas's little boy, as it so happens.

' "Is your dad in, o'but?"

' "No. Him yunt here, mister. Him went out when our mam came in. Her was in a bit of a hurry, thou's see."

'Well, a didn't see, but no matter. It looked as though Thomas could do with a feow of them educational books. Ignorant sod.

' "Well, is your mam in, then?"

' "No. Her had to go out when my uncle came in."

'Well, 'a thought, this is a bloody funny house. And why does he kip me waiting on the doorstep?

' "Is your Uncle in then, boy?" ' (said with more exasperation).

' "No. Him went out when my sister came in."

' "Well, surely to Christ your sister's in then? Eh?"'

' "No. Her yunt. Her went out when I came in."'

'Him couldn't stand any more of this. "Well, what sart of house is this then, o'but. Seem a bit queer to me."'

' "This yunt our house" ' (Cyril made the boy's voice with infinite contempt). ' "This is the shit house. Our house is up the garden." '

I have no idea whether this crude little story reads as anything but that, since I can hear Cyril's voice and mimicry, with the variations in the speed of telling. The stranger had been discomfited. The children present all appeared to love it, as much as their parents, and, after more jokes and mimicry, Cyril was given the loudest round of applause of the lot. 'I'll Take You Home Again Kathleen' and 'The Happy Wanderer' followed, sounding, at this late stage, as though the music had been rubbed inside the body of an empty, froth-speckled beer glass and then held up to be dried by a hundred throaty blasts. Some of those in the Club had perhaps had too much to drink by now, and were talking with an earnestness which needed a terrible concentration of face and eyes.

The scene described above might well seem drab enough, an alcoholic interlude inserted in the book suspiciously like repetitive 'atmosphere' or cut-aways in a poor documentary film just before the interviewer snaps his hard eyes at those who hum and haw over his questions. And I'm not sure that it would have been pretty dull if you did not know any of the people and thus found it difficult to respond to the various ripples circling out from the small number of communal centres which make up the social life of any working village.

When pamphleteers and lecturers talk of 'working-class culture' in order to rebut the work of people like Richard Hoggart and Raymond Williams (I am, perhaps, thinking specifically of Richard Wollheim whose intelligent, courteous and exceptionally well-argued pieces on this theme nevertheless seem to me to be totally unsympathetic not only to what experience makes one understand of the term but also to the differing strands of feeling and legitimate – in my opinion 'legitimate', but that's a nerve – aspiration which operate within what is called 'working-class culture'. But this is not the place to pursue such points), they take their stands on the superiority of a particular and limited academic culture, which is only middle-class in the sense that it largely belongs to a small minority in that class, and, on these terms, find the apparent paucity of working-class standards.

And here, in the Club and other local centres, there is little or no talk of Wesker or Osborne or Joan Littlewood (there *might* be about *Noel Coward*), and the external culture comes from the telly, and mostly from commercial television: on the whole, I think, television that is dreary, repetitive, sordid, commercial and second-rate. It is with the links to culture in the sense of 'the best that is said and done, and has been said and done' that one can see a genuine form of social poverty in English life. And, not only are the links tenuous, many of them have been deliberately snapped off, for reasons of money, other people's money, and the building of glass offices with a painting in the board room. There is, here, little acknowledgement of the force and vitality of such a 'heritage', and, where it is partially recognized, it is rejected as an intrusion because of the stale, sickly smell of class and condescension which seems inseparable from the condition of England. But, at the risk of being obvious, 'culture' in the proper sense is descriptive of a texture of living and of *change* – it is, of course, a political term, and explains conflict, exploitation, deprivation and aspiration within the history and the potentiality of a community, and, naturally, is not simply a matter of 'intellect' and the sensibilities of the 'educated'.

I digress because working-class culture is not to be written of in the past tense (as Wollheim writes of it, for instance), nor is it to be abandoned, Dwight Macdonald style, as the empty, sterile thing suggested by the controllers and some of their touts in the mass media, nor is it the *opposite* of the more cognitive, academic and leisured parts of a middle-class culture. If you wanted to caricature it, to swoop in on it with a dateline, a camera and a significant Sunday-paper headline, then it might easily appear the clownish and brutish thing it is so frequently assumed (with the best will in the world) to be. In fact, we rarely do see or read anything that is not a caricature of the way the great majority of our people live. For me, the ultimate degeneration happens when scraps of observation, mere fragments unrelated to any whole conception or experience, are presented as comments on our cultural situation, as proof of the dead-eyed, inert apathy of the people and, sooner or later, as justifications for a 'culture' which is safely based on hierarchies of social position and educational attainment. In a changing political situation, with new sources of power and new means of exploitation, new kinds of poverty, we seem to have lost the ability to leap these barriers, and can find little satisfaction on either side of them: the 'pop' culture, entangled as it must be with pre-pop functions and materials, with the older, more firmly based and collective responses of the working class on the one side, and the Sunday critics, Monitor, hush, hush, hushed on the other, chinking light refracted through brandy glasses.

I want to be cautious, and I am on dangerous ground: the evenings like the one described are becoming fewer and fewer in the Club. The Entertainments Committee has decided to stop piano playing on the normal week-end nights, to allow time for records and housey-housey. The fruit machines whirr (they really do whirr) and the records click as they change. Housey-housey, or Bingo, its other name, is played for hours, and with great enthusiasm. The set-piece concert parties have all but disappeared, and the television is on more often. There is, too, less 'visiting' in the village, more buses, more dances, more concern about school examinations. The secondary modern schoolchildren, as well as those at the grammar school, wear uniform. Each time I return, I feel a number of subtle changes – a few pretentious wrought-iron gates, a thick platform of brothel-creeper to walk on, another juke-box, an emptier club, a miner at a wedding in a top hat, a number of blazers with meaningless crests, a tut-tutting about other people's strikes, a change of newspapers in the letter box, a house given a new name.

These are the small things, but each time, also, I feel a shift of values, the unrest of the anxiety behind the change. I feel the decline of the distinctive Forest culture, not so much in the healthy and necessary senses, but in the almost neurotic turning aside from the label 'working class' and from the older loyalties. Part of this may well be inevitable in any situation of rapid change, but more of it, I regret, is due to the meaningless nature of 'choice' between the older values and the newer, brighter, corroding uniformity of the new so-called post capitalism.

Certainly, one can say with absolute confidence that the settings here have changed. There has been no sharpness about this, though the most important changes have come well within a single adulthood. If we had an all-seeing camera taking a huge number of impressions over a decade or so, the scenes would naturally mix into each other with almost pointless similarity until, suddenly, in retrospect, we would realize that the last pictures we see would have been strange and worrying to the people in the earlier impressions. Take out an old photograph and you have the uncanny sensation that something has interfered with it, that the figures in it are holding their heads differently, that they have other expressions stilled on to their faces, other tunes running through their minds. The 'past', when discovered in this way, seems unrelated to the present: we see only the funny women's fashions, hear the unappropriate slang, and get a total impression which makes it all seem so long, long ago, easily separable from the moods and feelings of here and now. Faded newspapers, or the popular songs of a decade or two ago have a touch and rhythm which is safe, old hat, neatly packaged. But in the streets of a working-class town or village, in the minds of the miner and the mother, the past does not seem so quaint and manageable, less a thing for the gentle sigh and the lowered eye of sentimental scrapbook-style recognition. Instead it is there as a physical thing, eaten away in places by the hollowed caverns of chain stores and pop-record shelves, boxed around by rows of neat new houses with pastel-coloured curtains over their clear, flat windows, and cloaked by the dress, style and conversations of people in the streets. But it still reaches out and threatens.

That is why one should be cautious.

An old man recently wrote an angry letter to the *Dean Forest Guardian*. 'I came to the Forest first some sixty-five years ago as a small boy . . . then the area was rich in brass bands, male voice and mixed choirs . . . and the pubs open till very late at night. Incidentally, the street pavements on Sunday morning were often foul with sickness, and interfering policemen liable to be met with bricks (I remember one being killed). A time when a football match between the two largest towns ended, as if by ritual, in a general fight. When men had to walk to work for miserable wages, in all weathers. When the main roads were deep in dust in summer and mud in winter. When councils thought wistfully of water schemes and sewage systems which existed only in their dreams. When typhoid was an ever-present threat and often a dread reality.' He had remembered too well, and was therefore excusing and praising the present too greatly. It has become too difficult to judge with angry-young-man glibness, but not too satisfactory or sufficiently just to avoid polemic. People are relaxing now, taking all they think they can get, but still not getting enough of what, without a giggle, I will call the good life.

But the Forest of Dean is an interesting and often a beautiful part of the country, so why not go and see for yourself? You will be struck by the differences it still has from the areas surrounding it, and by the sounds of the speech there. Only gradually will you notice that, as elsewhere, things are out of focus. Conversation has not always caught up with the change, and many of those involved in the older pursuits do so for different reasons than formerly, and a young man who plays rugby keeps sliding into the past tense when talking of his team or his village. In what may appear the drizzle of small-scale change, you will ultimately discover that a whole pattern is being submerged, and that the new, far from being distinct, is familiar in every high street and newspaper advertisement.

'Blessed is the eye, that rests between the Severn and the Wye,' they will still insist on telling you. I love the place very much, and in many ways that are not at all sentimental or romantic, I find it difficult to separate many of its values and qualities from the ideas, memories and expectations which are part of my own personality. I think, too, that there is much in the Forest of Dean which will not be hammered flat, and which will not make one despair of hoping for Change which is less destructive and more emancipating than that which we have experienced. At the very least, if you visit there, you will find yourself part of a strongly bound community, and some of the power of it will rub off. It may be that you will feel then that I have exaggerated 'change', that I have taken my title too seriously, but I do not think so.